PENTABUS
RURAL THEATRE COMPAN

A Pentabus Theatre Company and
Everyman Theatre Cheltenham production

WOLVES ARE COMING FOR YOU

by Joel Horwood

Wolves Are Coming For You was first performed at
Bromfield Village Hall, Shropshire, on 27 September 2017

Wolves Are Coming For You

by Joel Horwood

Cast

ONE	Helena Lymbery
TWO	Stacey Evans

Creative Team

Director	Sophie Motley
Designer	Carla Goodman
Composer/Sound Designer	Peter Power
Lighting Designer	Azusa Ono
Movement Director	Kitty Winter
Production Manager	Tammy Rose
Technical Manager	Sam Eccles
Touring Stage Manager	Oran O'Neill

Special thanks to:

Elizabeth Freestone, Anthony Haighway, Mary-Lou McCarthy,
Paul Milton, Katherine Pearce, Sarah-Jane Shiels, Adam Wall,
Anne Haydock, Richard Burbidge, Colonel David Lewis, Sarah Leigh.

Tour Dates 2017

27 September | Bromfield Village Hall | Shropshire
28 September | Bromfield Village Hall | Shropshire
29 September | Presteigne Assembly Rooms | Powys
30 September | Leintwardine Community Centre | Herefordshire

4–7 October | Everyman Theatre Cheltenham Studio | Gloucestershire

11 October | Hereford College | Herefordshire
12 October | Sundial Theatre | Gloucestershire
13 October | Cliffords Mesne Village Hall | Gloucestershire
14 October | Quatt Village Hall | Shropshire

18 October | Ombersley Memorial Hall | Worcestershire
19 October | Swythamley & Heaton Community Centre | Staffordshire
20 October | Clows Top Victory Hall | Worcestershire
21 October | Broadbent Theatre | Lincolnshire

25 October | Courtyard | Yorkshire
26 October | The Reading Room | County Durham
27 October | Yarm School | Yorkshire
28 October | Danby Village Hall | Yorkshire

2 November | Kirkby Stephen Sports & Social Club | Cumbria
3 November | The Brewery | Cumbria
4 November | Castle Eden Village Hall | County Durham

CAST

Helena Lymbery | ONE
Theatre includes: *Harry Potter and the Cursed Child* (Palace, West End); *Treasure Island, We Want You to Watch, Women of Troy, The Cat in the Hat, This House, Attempts on Her Life, Some Trace of Her, Iphigenia at Aulis, His Dark Materials* (National Theatre); *Rough Cuts: God Bless the Child* (Royal Court); *Yerma* (West Yorkshire Playhouse); *Watership Down* (Lyric Hammersmith); *Blue Remembered Hills* (New Victoria); *My Sister in This House* (Theatr Clwyd); *The Woman Who Swallowed a Pin* (Southwark Playhouse); *Digging for Ladies* (Amy Roadstone: open air tour); *The Asylum Project* (Riverside Studios); *Mammals* (Bush).

Television includes: *Doctor Foster, Oliver Twist, The Bill, Oranges and Lemons, Inspector Lynley Mysteries.*

Film includes: *London Road.*

Stacey Evans | TWO
Stacey left Guildford School of Acting with the Graduate Acting Award and has subsequently worked in film, television and theatre.
Her recent work includes: *Kids in Love* (Ealing Studios); *Seat 25* (winner of Best British Film at the London Film Awards and Best Feature Film at Birmingham Film Festival). Theatre includes: *Vernon God Little* (Burn Bright); *The Wedding Reception* (2017 Edinburgh run for Interactive Theatre International); *Blitz, Shelter* (Nuffield); *Anne of Green Gables, The Phoenix and the Carpet, Free Folk* by award-winning playwright Gary Owen (Forest Forge). Stacey also writes and films her own comedy sketches and occasionally attempts to perform stand-up comedy.

.

CREATIVE TEAM

Joel Horwood | Writer

Joel is a playwright, director and dramaturg, and is a creative associate at the Lyric Hammersmith theatre in London.

Theatre: *Food* (The Imaginary Body); *Stoopud F*cken Animals* (Traverse); *Is Everyone OK?* (nabokov); *I Caught Crabs in Walberswick, I ♥ Peterborough* (Eastern Angles); *The Planet and Stuff* (Polka/Tonic); *A Series of Increasingly Impossible Acts* (Lyric Hammersmith); *I Want My Hat Back* (National Theatre); *The Little Matchgirl and Other Happier Tales* (Shakespeare's Globe).

Radio: *Ok Computer* (Radio 4).

Sophie Motley | Director

Sophie studied at the Samuel Beckett Centre, Trinity College, Dublin, and trained on Rough Magic's SEEDS 3 and the National Theatre Studio Director's programme. She founded WillFredd Theatre Company and was Associate Director of Rough Magic in Dublin.

Recent directing work includes: *Millions of Years* (ENO Baylis); *BEES!, Jockey, Care, Follow, Farm* (WillFredd Theatre); *Tejas Verdes, Vincent River* (Prime Cut); *The Sleeping Queen* (Wexford Festival Opera); *Everything Between Us, Plaza Suite* (Rough Magic). Sophie was Staff Director at English National Opera, Resident Assistant Director at the Abbey Theatre and Associate Director and Dramaturg with Michel van der Aa / Dutch National Opera.

Carla Goodman | Designer

Carla trained in Nottingham, London and New York.

Recent design credits include, for Pentabus: *As the Crow Flies*. Previous: *Gabriel* (Richmond/UK tour); *Pride and Prejudice, What Flows Past the Baltic* (Nottingham Playhouse); *Looking at Lucian* (Ustinov Bath); *Jack and the Beanstalk* (Cast); *How to Date a Feminist* (Arcola); *Exposure, Pig Farm* (St James); *Rise* (Old Vic Outdoors); *Miss Julie* (Etcetera); *Not Moses* (Arts); *Romeo and Juliet* (Orange Tree); *Heartbreak Hotel* (The Jetty, Greenwich); *Truce* (New Wimbledon); *Theatre Uncut* (Traverse/UK tour); *Listen, We're Family* (Wilton's Music Hall); *Ariodante* (Royal Academy of Music); *Miss Nightingale* (Lowry/UK tour); *Mush and Me* (Bush).

Upcoming work includes: *Joy* (Stratford East) and *The Nutcracker* (Cornerstone Arts Centre).

Peter Power | Composer/Sound Designer

Peter Power is a Composer, Sound Designer and Director from Waterford, based in Cork. Peter's current and recent projects include: *Neon Western* (Conflicted Theatre); *The Same* by Enda Walsh (Corcadorca); *ProdiJIG the Revolution* (Cork Opera House); *Override* by the award-winning Stacey Gregg (Dublin Fringe Festival) and the commissioned work *fLux* (Eat My Noise for Cork Film Festival).

Peter is currently embarking on a self-directed residency with the National Sculpture Factory of Ireland supported by the Arts Council of Ireland. This residency will be about exploring the intersections of Visual Arts and Composition, culminating in a 10-piece modular work entitled *Versations* in 2019.

Previous residencies include Hotel Pro Forma in Denmark as part of their Atelier in 2014, an international art lab for young, recognised and international artists to develop work created across art forms and MAKE in the Tyrone Guthrie Centre in 2015.

Peter is also Director of Eat My Noise, a multi-genre audio collective that work in event, film, television and production. Most recently Peter has composed and directed Eat My Noise's work *Carinae*, presented as part of Sounds from a Safe Harbour Festival. Other projects include: *Inquyre* for Cork Film Festival; *Moeity & A:Volution* for Cork Midsummer Festival; *Spindle* for Big House Festival; *Gentrification* and *How These Desperate Men Talk* by Enda Walsh, co-productions with Corcadorca. Eat My Noise also compose works for TG4, RTÉ and RTÉ2 as part of various documentaries, televisions series and short film.

Peter holds a degree in Biochemistry and a Masters in Composition and Electronics from University College Cork.

Azusa Ono | Lighting Designer

Azusa trained in fine art in Japan and lighting design at the Central School of Speech and Drama in London.

Recent design credits include: *Kairos* (V&A Museum); *Becoming Invisible* (Bascule Chamber-Tower Bridge); *Smack That* (national tour); *Killer* (Shoreditch Town Hall); *Darkness Darkness* (Nottingham Playhouse); *Cuttin' It* (Young Vic/national tour); *The Tiger's Bones and Other Stories* (Nottingham Lakeside/national tour); *I Know All The Secrets In My World* (Derby/tour); *Dot, Squiggle and Rest* (Royal Opera House – Clore Studio); *Peddling* (New York 59E59/national tour); *Playland* (Derby/national tour); *How Nigeria Became a Story and a Spear that Didn't Work* (Unicorn); *We Are Proud…* (Bush); *The Lovesong of Alfred J Hitchcock* (Curve, Leicester/international tour); *Copyright Christmas* (Barbican); *Fanfared* (Crucible Sheffield); *Choreogata* (Southbank Centre – Purcell Room).

Website: www.ald.org.uk/azusaono

Kitty Winter | Movement Director

Kitty Winter is a movement director, choreographer and director, she trained at Laban and on the MA Movement course at the Central School of Speech and Drama.

Recent movement credits include: *The Kite Runner* (Wyndham's/Playhouse/national tour); *Alice in Wonderland, Cinderella, A Christmas Carol, The Rise and Fall of Little Voice* (Derby); *As The Crow Flies, Here I Belong* (Pentabus); *Blood* (Tamasha/Belgrade Coventry); *Rapunzel, Jack* (Nottingham Playhouse); *Tiny Treasures, The Night Pirates* (Theatre Hullabaloo); *The Dog House, Women on the Verge of HRT, Puss in Boots* (Derby LIVE); *Swan Canaries* (Arletty); *The Magical Playroom* (Seabright Productions/Pleasance Edinburgh); *Roots* (Mercury, Colchester); *Gandhi and Coconuts* (Kali/Arcola); *Dick Turpin's Last Ride* (Theatre Royal Bury St Edmunds) and *Squid* (Theatre Royal Stratford East).

Recent directing credits include: *Feet First* and *Car Story* (Box Clever); *Spinning Yarns, FIVE* (Theatre Hullabaloo/Theatre Direct, Canada); *The Blue Moon* (Wriggle Dance Theatre); *Anything to Declare?* (The Gramophones); *Whose Shoes?* (Nottingham Playhouse) and *Awaking Durga* (Kali/Soho).

Kitty is Co-Artistic Director of family theatre company WinterWalker, and has recently produced and directed *The Nutcracker and the Mouse King* (Lincoln Drill Hall & Déda, Derby); *Three Keepers* (UK tour); *Come to the Circus* (Déda, Derby); and *The Beast of Belper* (Belper Arts Festival). You can find out more about her work at **www.kittywinter.com**

PENTABUS
RURAL THEATRE COMPANY

We are the nation's rural theatre company.

We develop, produce and tour new plays to village halls, fields, communities and theatres, telling stories with local relevance and national impact.

Since 1974 Pentabus has produced over 160 new plays, supported over 100 playwrights and reached nearly a million audience members. We've won awards, pioneered live-streaming and developed a groundbreaking initiative to nurture young writers from rural backgrounds.

Our plans for the future will see us tour to far-flung rural communities, work with new and established artists and playwrights, extend our young writers' programme and continue to push at the boundaries of what theatre can be.

Pentabus is a registered charity (number 287909). We rely on the generosity of our donors, small and large, to help us to make brilliant new theatre.

You can find out more about us at **www.pentabus.co.uk**

Artistic Director	Sophie Motley
Managing Director	Kitty Ross
Producer	Jenny Pearce
Development Manager	Francesca Spickernell
Development Officer	Georgina Sharp
Administrator	Alice Samuels
Audience Development Consultant	Verity Overs-Morell
Technical Manager	Sam Eccles
Bookkeeper	Lynda Lynne
Associate Artist	Tim Foley
Volunteers	Mike Price, Stephen Abbott, Ian Yarroll

Twitter @pentabustheatre
Facebook Pentabus Theatre
Instagram pentabustheatrecompany

Pentabus Theatre Company, Bromfield, Ludlow, Shropshire, SY8 2JU

Pentabus is also supported by The Millichope Foundation

EVERYMAN
THEATRE · CHELTENHAM

The Everyman Theatre, Cheltenham, is one of the country's leading performance venues, hosting pre- and post-West End productions. It also creates its own work, both in the 700-seat Main House and in the intimate Studio Theatre. The Everyman has a large Education and Community Department, which works in school settings, colleges, the University of Gloucestershire and communities throughout the county.

Each year the Everyman co-produces and commissions up to eight new pieces of work. In 2017 this includes *Sofa* (dementia-themed play) with the Makeshift Ensemble, *The Wind in the Willows* with Box Tale Soup, *Twenty-One Pounds* (a new play about slavery by Martin Lytton), *Comedy Chekhov* with Bridge Theatre Company, *Baby Blues* with Forthright Theatre, *Tales from Hans Christian Andersen* and *A Gloucestershire Midwinter* with Hammerpuzzle and *Wolves Are Coming For You* with Pentabus Theatre Company.

The Everyman's Project Brain is a four-year body of artistic and community work exploring the human brain and related neurological conditions. Working with a range of partners, from health practitioners and specialists, to schools and groups, the project runs in Dementia Homes, Day Centres, Community Venues and in the Everyman Theatre itself. Partners on Project Brain include P3, imove and Theatre Temoin.

In addition to its school and college work, the Everyman runs networking and training sessions for mid-career performers and creatives. The Actors' Lab, which has been running for fifteen years, comprises workshops for professional performers based in the South West. The Writers' Lab trains playwrights and occasionally commissions work by its members for production in the Studio Theatre. The Practitioners' Lab trains workshop leaders who may progress to work in the Everyman's education and community pool of practitioners.

| Chief Executive | Mark Goucher |
| Creative Director | Paul Milton |

www.everymantheatre.org.uk

WOLVES ARE COMING FOR YOU

Joel Horwood

for Nic and Helen

Thanks to

Maria Aberg
Kasper Aberg Horwood
Hugh Colville
Elizabeth Freestone
Jay Griffiths
Anthony Haighway
Serena Mason
Mary-Lou McCarthy
Sophie Motley
Pete Musthill
Kat Pearce
Pope
Sarah-Jane Shiels
Rachel Taylor

And special thanks to the town of Presteigne

'An enemy is someone whose story you have not heard.'

Irene Butter

Author's Note

This play was conceived and written for two women to perform, but it can be presented with as many actors as you see fit. In order to do so, however, it is important to empower larger companies with my thinking – both in terms of writing for female performers and of writing for two performers – so that you can adapt the text as needed.

In the community in which I grew up, the matriarchs were the storytellers. Stories are how we discuss, investigate, attempt to define ourselves, our history, our future. As storytellers, women are the guardians of the identity of a community. They shape the minds of the newer generations, they tend the bewildered older generations, they shepherd their communities through endless change with the comfort of structured narrative. So I wrote *Wolves Are Coming For You* for two women to steer the audience through each unique show, through the imaginative process of change that occurs within the village of the play.

It is written for two actors because themes of performance are essential to the play. The text collides performance techniques (audience interaction, actor's invention, direct address, near-naturalism, constant doubling, physicality); certain lines concern identity itself as a performance; the ritual of storytelling is a subject of the play. In order to achieve the clarity of storytelling that this play requires, the actors must be virtuosic in their differentiation of each character. This was all in the hope that our audiences would engage in the game of identifying signifiers of difference; for example, they might recognise that ONE is playing BEA because they notice her hand tremor. However, the hope is that they will never lose sight of 'ONE'. So they will almost accidentally engage in the game of investigating just how facile some of those differences are. The hope is that these two performers will tacitly imply that we are all very similar, very frightened, very hopeful animals.

Bearing this in mind, please use and abuse this text as you see fit. Adapt the Prologue and Epilogue to create two 'sort of' narrators, share the lines you need around your entire company, or none of the above. Whatever works for you. Will we meet your actors as themselves in the 'pre-show'? Or see them pull on costumes or make-up? I hope you enjoy finding your own way to perform this particular little ritual.

J.H.

Characters

ONE
TWO
ANNA
BEA
CHRIS
DEE
ELLEN
FERDY
GRACE
HARRY
EMMA-LOU
POPE
KING
MEL
IDA

Production Note

This play relies on its audience. In the Prologue, the audience are invited to participate, to collaborate with the play, to imaginatively transform our actors and their surroundings to serve the story. This idea could be pulled through every creative decision regarding the production; from design to acting, everything. This event could feel like a unique collaboration. And I hope that this script and this production note also leave room for you to collaborate with the ideas too.

In the Prologue, 'TWO' has a line thanking someone for the use of the room. This is because this play has been conceived to be performed in village halls. This may need adjusting depending on the performance space. This change will need to also affect the final line of the play.

The doubling could be as follows:

ONE – *Bea, Dee, Ferdy, Harry, Emma-Lou, Mel*

TWO – *Anna, Chris, Ellen, Grace, Pope, King, Ida*

A forward slash (/) in the text marks the point at which the next speaker interrupts.

This text went to press before the end of rehearsals and so may differ slightly from the play as performed.

Prologue

We create a warm and welcoming atmosphere. Perhaps there's music. Perhaps the performers welcome the audience.

Our actors could create a preparatory ritual for themselves – it can be as small as a handshake or a few moments of eye contact – the important thing is that it is for the two performers and it occurs moments before the first written line. This line:

ONE. Are we all here? Everyone ready?

Maybe there's a response, maybe not.

Okay. Thank you for joining us for tonight's performance of *Wolves Are Coming For You*. And thanks especially to – [*name of FOH or village-hall manager*] for organising everything so that we could be here with you now. My name's – [*name*] and this is – [*name*].

TWO. Yes. Hello. The scenes of our play take place over twenty-four hours in and around a village. Various locations, various characters. So, no traditional set.

TWO *begins to shake out some soil to create a circular patch of earth.*

ONE. Which means we need you. We need you to fill in the gaps far more than a nice bit of painted background might. We need you to entirely transform this room. To change this floor into the cold stone of a church if needs be, or the mulch of an old forest. To recreate this ceiling and make for us the low beams of a village pub or explode it into a canopy of stars if that's the setting. This is me inviting, summoning, conjuring you to help us.

TWO. We do also have some lights and sound, operated by – [*name*] at the back there.

This person waves.

ONE. The first scene is set just before dawn. So, the stars fading as the sky brightens. Mist puddling in the shallow of the valley. The sun hasn't broken the brow of the hill over there but it's coming. It looks how it must have looked when all this was truly, properly, wild. Doesn't it?

TWO. Basic layout. Up here on the hill, Lewis Farm. It's almost always been there, always with a Lewis working it. It's even in the Doomsday Book with the same name but now, Bea Lewis runs it alone. She's in her late seventies. Her only daughter, Anna, no interest in farming. At all. She's driving here from that direction, the city, power ballads on the radio, practising the things she wants to say to her mother when she arrives. Things like, 'I thought we could have breakfast together, got some parma ham, sourdough – No, the sheep can wait, I *insist*.' And things like, 'Well, you must have noticed it yourself, Mum – No. Whether you've noticed or not, Mum, we need to talk about it.' That's Anna Lewis. Downhill from Lewis Farm is the church, the churchyard, the rectory where the vicar lives.

ONE. His name is Christopher. He's in his bed, talking to himself in his sleep. I say talking, more accurately, he's making a reassuring sound. A sound like this…

TWO. Hm.

ONE. Repeatedly.

TWO. Hm.

ONE. His wife, Dee, teaches in the school in our village –

TWO. Hm.

ONE. So, as usual, Dee is downstairs with piles of marking, not asleep.

TWO. Graveyard spreads downhill, backs onto the school playing field. Small school, they're trying to close it. A handful of houses over here, 'The Street' it's called, then there's the pub, obviously, always a pub, called…?

Maybe there's a response, maybe not.

Thank you. Then a few even older cottages, the new estate was built just over there, not many houses, and a small wood between them and the village proper. Stream here, bridge, green and village hall.

ONE. No one knows this but the hall at the heart of the village is built on the remains of an ancient church. And that church was built on a church that might have been Norse. And that was built on the site of a Roman church. Which was built on a pagan church. Which was built where fires used to be. Fires around which people would gather for food, warmth, to dance perhaps, to discuss threats, peace, the future, the past. Stories. No one knows that this has always been a place for stories, no one knows any of this.

TWO. So beyond the village hall, one road heads for the bypass, that way, that's 'New Road', built about fifty years ago, and the other heads off to another village, similar, but worlds apart.

ONE. The people who live here, they're people like me. Maybe a bit like you. People with responsibilities, parents, pets, children, memories of first kisses and deep losses, health problems, hopes, fears... Good people. Some of them might be taller than I am, shorter, thinner, fatter, older, younger, darker, lighter, they might have accents different to our own. The vicar, for example, Christopher.

TWO. Hm.

ONE. He's middle-aged, rarely exercises so looks comfortable, he has bags under his eyes in spite of sleeping well. The local policeman, Harry, tends to stand a bit like this. It doesn't feel natural to him, it just helps him feel like he's less himself and more his job.

TWO. Ferdy lives in a caravan in the woods, dreadlocks, about six-foot-four, skin darker than this. Suffers from night terrors. Only, he suffers from them in the daytime too. They lurk in the shadows and make him –

ONE *shows us* FERDY, *flinching suddenly, thinking he's seen something in the woods.*

Ellen tends to talk quickly, and say 'yeah, no, yeah, like, yeah' a lot. She's in her teens and overweight, two things that can change a school playground into a war zone. Her mother, Grace. Grace tends to say that her daughter is, 'A bit fragile, under lots of pressure, the best thing I can do is make sure she's happy at home.' Grace bakes cakes for Ellen, every day, and Ellen eats them, every day, because Grace measures their relationship in food.

ONE. Which is something Dee is concerned about. Dee is the vicar's wife –

TWO. Hm.

ONE. Yes, she's Christopher's wife and she is Ellen's teacher. So, at the most recent parents' evening, Dee tried to discuss Ellen's weight with Grace. But her attempt went something like: 'Grace, your daughter is a wonderful learner, she's absorbing so much from you, strong beliefs, you know, school council, but... Well, she doesn't like sports or engage in the, um... She hates the changing rooms... and... about the cakes... Could I get a copy of some of the recipes?'

TWO. But now, it's just before sunrise, Anna's driving home to Lewis Farm up on the hill, the radio on, practising her lines. 'Getting older, it happens to us all, it's a natural thing.'

ONE. She's turned off the bypass, wound her way along the 'New Road' into our village, passed the village hall and, on her way up the hill, thrown a glance into the shallow valley. Mist puddling, sky brightening, stars fading as the sun just about breaks the brow of the hill.

TWO. 'It's a perfectly natural thing to happen to... And we just need to... Manage it together.'

Slowly, we fade up 'Eye of the Tiger' by Survivor.

ONE. Turning up the bumpy lane towards Lewis's farmhouse, Anna doesn't know that Bea's already awake. Bea Lewis woke when she felt someone touch her hand. She woke from a dream about being knee-deep in mud, slipping, sliding down into a mucky, dark hole, nothing to grip. Looking down, in her dream, she felt someone above her grasp her hand, someone she knew to be her late husband, wanting to help. That's when she woke up. And now she's made herself a cup of tea, the same hand still shaking, trembling, like this. And she hears something outside...

TWO. Pulling into the yard, Anna sees her mother stood in the headlights. She turns off 'Eye of the Tiger' and wants to say something as she steps out of the car but her mum beats her to it, Bea says –

ACT ONE

1.

5:13 a.m.

BEA. Wolf.

ANNA. Sorry?

BEA. Wolf, Anna.

ANNA. Mum –

BEA. Saw it.

ANNA. Okay. Okay, um... A, er, a wolf?

BEA. Yep.

ANNA. You saw –

BEA. Coming for the lambs. Not normally alone, are they?

ANNA. No they're not – It's just, bit of a surprising welcome after a long drive, this.

BEA. So? This is livestock.

ANNA. Sure, okay, yeah –

BEA. Saw it just now.

ANNA. Right.

BEA. Must be more coming or already about.

ANNA. Right. You're serious, you're telling me you've just seen a – a – ?

BEA. Wolf.

ANNA. Okay, so... where was this?

BEA. Here.

ANNA. Here?

BEA. There.

ANNA. So, first things first, Mum, it's really early –

BEA. Not for me.

ANNA. You must be half-asleep.

BEA. Not early for a farmer.

ANNA. No, but for a woman who's almost eighty –

BEA. Not early for animals, wolves.

ANNA. Still, I thought we could have breakfast together, I can make some coffee –

BEA. Breakfast?

ANNA. Yeah, parma ham, sourdough, I *insist*, the sheep can wait –

BEA. You mad? I've got livestock –

ANNA. Okay, okay. So you were just up and about in your wellies, your nightie, and you thought you saw –

BEA. *Thought* I saw?

ANNA. Yeah, can we actually just go in? Just for a minute, it's been a long drive –

BEA. In? Now?

ANNA. It's cold and you're – Yes 'in now', Mum, can you hear yourself?

BEA. You go in, I'm not.

ANNA. Can we not start like this? Please? Not immediately at each other's throats, all teeth and fangs.

BEA. Don't look at me like that, then.

ANNA. Like what?

BEA. Like I'm at the bottom of some hole.

ANNA. Right, okay, let's... okay, where did you see this... this wolf, you saw it just now, yes?

BEA. Headlights.

ANNA. My headlights? Mum?

BEA. You didn't see it.

ANNA. No. I didn't see it.

BEA. I did.

ANNA. Well, I didn't –

BEA. Not used to seeing things, you. Not used to it.

ANNA. Let's have a cup of tea, talk about this properly?

BEA. Talking won't help my lambs.

ANNA. At least put something warmer on –

BEA. You don't decide things for me.

ANNA. I know that.

BEA. Can't feel cold when those things are after my lambs, there's a nation to feed!

ANNA. Ugh –

BEA. More than income, this. It's in my veins, yours too –

ANNA. Will you just put a coat on – ?

BEA. No!

ANNA. Right, you saw it in my headlights, yes? In the direction of my car – ? Where I came from, that's where you think more wolves will be coming from, is it? Cos – Shall we just, let's just be a little realistic, shall we? Think about the facts, for a minute.

BEA. Facts are, heard it first, howling, came out and saw it in your headlights.

ANNA. Okay. Okay, well, alternative facts might include: the fact it's not very light, there are foxes, badgers –

BEA. Wasn't a fox –

ANNA. No, but –

BEA. Think I am?

ANNA. Yeah, okay, but you may also have. Heard the music I was playing and maybe that somehow added to the confusion or –

BEA. I work this land, it's what I do, these eyes, this body, me.
Know a dog from a fox from music from a wolf from a
daughter, I know these things.

ANNA. What's more likely, Mum? You saw an actual real wolf
or that you *projected* your, I don't know, concerns, maybe?
Upon seeing me, maybe because there's something I might
bring up, something you're afraid of –

BEA. Not listening to this –

ANNA. Seeing things from my perspective, finding you out
here, dressed like this –

BEA. Not listening –

ANNA. What's most likely? Wolf or, you know, *imagined* wolf?

BEA. Are you saying something's wrong with me?

ANNA....no, not –

BEA. How would you know? Hey?

ANNA. I'm not –

BEA. Why would I believe you and not how I feel?

ANNA (*carefully*). Some diseases –

BEA. Getting the shotgun.

ANNA. No, Mum – Shotgun? Just wait until it's properly light
at least, stop being so –

BEA. Strong, is what I'm being. Strong like you wouldn't
know. You'd do the same if there was a danger, real danger
to – to your own, your livestock, if you knew, if you knew
what it felt like –

ANNA. If I knew what – ?

BEA. What family felt like.

ANNA. Right. Great. Thanks, Mum, that's –

BEA. You don't know the strength I've got.

ANNA. Oh, I know your strength.

BEA. I protect my stock.

ANNA. You think cruelty's the same as strength.

BEA. *Me*, cruel? *Me?*

ANNA. Mum, we have to talk –

BEA. I've got livestock to think of –

ANNA. Fine, well, I'm not leaving so –

BEA. Neither am I!

ANNA. I'm here *for* you, Mum, so we can make a plan / together.

BEA. When's the last time you got yourself laid?

2.

7:47 a.m.

BEA. Not proud of it. Sorry, to repeat it here. But it's what I said.

CHRIS. The last time she got herself...?

BEA. Laid.

CHRIS. Hm.

BEA. Sex. It means sex, Vicar.

CHRIS. And this is something you're... concerned about, the last time your daughter had – ?

BEA. No.

CHRIS. Hm... Well, families are a safe place, sometimes to give vent, to say things we don't mean –

BEA. I meant it. Meant to hurt her.

CHRIS. Mm. Well, losing control –

BEA. Didn't lose control. I don't lose control.

CHRIS. Hm. Well, is Anna staying for any length of time? Did she head straight off?

BEA. No. She's either in bed up there. Or eating her posh ham and avo-bloody-cado.

CHRIS. Well, then, there's time to... to apologise and discuss –

BEA. Not apologising.

CHRIS. No?

BEA. Not for something I meant to say.

CHRIS. Hm.

An awkward pause develops. There's more that BEA *wants to say. And it's not what she says next.*

BEA. These are a terrible state. Should redo them, get Tony up here and redo them.

CHRIS. Redo the...

BEA. Flagstones. Can't read this one at all.

CHRIS. Well, it's the wear and tear of what was a very busy church, all those feet –

BEA. Can't be forgotten about, Vicar. Can they? He shouldn't charge you for it either, Tony, I'll speak to him, send him up here myself.

CHRIS. Hm.

Another pause develops. CHRIS *takes a punt.*

What I like about this church on mornings like this, early like this, is the smell. The still air. Old air. Makes me reflect on the nature of faith. Not just the faith of those buried here or those who laid these stones, one atop the other, to build all this, this spire. But on the faith of all the people who have breathed the air of this room then, since, now... (*Reading the floor.*) John, Margaret, Elizabeth... This air passed through their lungs, their bodies. It helped them to manage and cope with some perfectly natural problems. Problems not so dissimilar from our own, I imagine. I take it as a constant reminder that I am alive in this moment and that this moment affords me, daily, the chance to change, to forgive, to –

BEA. I'm not forgiving her, she's vicious. Cruel.

CHRIS. Hm. Still, she's here to visit you –

BEA. Not a visit. Not a friendly visit.

CHRIS. Hm. You see, it's my reading of the Bible that no one is inherently bad or good. We are simply reflected in the actions we –

BEA. Her actions are bad.

CHRIS. Hm.

BEA. She came here to… manage me.

CHRIS. Manage – ?

BEA. I don't smell what you smell in here. I smell… damp. Decay. Death.

CHRIS. Well, we all have darker days, those things are, in their own way, part of Creation –

BEA. What 'bad actions' have I done?

CHRIS. You?

BEA. I've done good. Worked hard. If there's no good or bad people, just good or bad actions, what actions have I done to deserve this?

CHRIS. To deserve, um – ?

BEA. I've worked. Every day of my life. Even the worst. I've worked.

CHRIS. Yes –

BEA. And I've been here. First in. Helping. Every time. Sometimes even when you haven't been here, I've been here putting the Bibles out. What did I do wrong?

CHRIS. Hm… um, well, 'wrong' is… You feel you're being, um… Ms Lewis, why are you asking this?

BEA *almost tells* CHRIS *everything but decides not to.*

BEA. Not the time or place.

CHRIS. Well, it is the place –

BEA. Mrs Russo will be in soon, she's normally here by now.

CHRIS. We don't speak often, do we? In fact, I think this is the most we've spoken in all these years. It seems you've chosen to speak now, so, this is the time and the place.

BEA....

CHRIS. It could be that this, um, is not a punishment, more a challenge or test. Opportunity. Something that invites us to connect with ourselves, with prayer. Perhaps it's in asking for help that we find the most appropriate, um... that we learn –

BEA. Killed my mother slowly. Forgot directions to start with. Then where she was. Then people. Who she was. Words went. Turned her feral. I was with her for all of it – Why do that to me? Hey?

CHRIS. Hm... Well... Um... Doubt lays the groundwork for faith so –

BEA. What do His actions say about Him?

CHRIS. About – ?

BEA. God. Why me – *me* – what does that say about Him?

CHRIS. Hm. Well...

BEA (*gesturing generally at herself*). Take this away, words, all of it. Turn me into... nothing, just teeth and fangs – *Me*. It's started too. You heard the howling, didn't you?

CHRIS. The, um...?

3.

10:18 a.m.

CHRIS. Wolves. With a straight face, she said this. Bea Lewis, old as the hills, shears and butchers her own sheep, grudges older than my church –

DEE. I know who she is, love.

CHRIS. She seriously believes she's turning into a wolf. I mean, it's not as wild as it all sounds, she's concerned she might have some progressive, aggressive, I don't know what, but it's clearly already leading to hallucinations – a wolf, she said, here, this morning – Even making the sound, you know, the –

DEE. Howling.

CHRIS. – wolves howling, yes, wanted to join in, she said, ran out. It's this disease, you see.

DEE. Second person today.

CHRIS. She's making sense of it by saying she's turning into – Sorry, did you say – ?

DEE. Ida O'Connell. She takes a short cut from the estate through the woods, said she saw one on her way in to school this morning.

CHRIS. A wolf?

DEE. Took her aside, talked about the power of stories, but nothing. Nothing at all.

CHRIS. Mm.

DEE. Perhaps you should do the same with Bea Lewis, love. Find a time, have a talk about rumours and / stories and such.

CHRIS. Sort of beside the point.

DEE. It's a control thing with Ida, you know her family, Dad's in prison, she's got that stammer on her S's, / you know, love.

CHRIS. This isn't what I asked you about, is it?

DEE. Christopher, I've got five minutes until the end of break. I was up with the marking, love, I need a cuppa or I'm no use to anyone. We can talk later on, okay?

CHRIS. Mm.

A short pause develops as CHRIS *notices something on his clothes and cleans it.* DEE *understands this little performance and interrupts.*

DEE. You know what I think? I think you could get yourself out in that garden, love, and have a go at that rock in the back with the weedkiller. Get the gloves on and root about in the beds, just forget about it for a while –

CHRIS. Weeds again, is it?

DEE. Yes, weeds again, always weeds, they're up there growing right now, pushing up, making a wilderness of our garden. I dream about those weeds, love. And the mould in the bathroom, and the ivy, it's all up the back wall –

CHRIS. Mm, Dee –

DEE. – that rhododendron that just won't die – They're on my mind constantly, Christopher –

CHRIS. I'm asking you –

DEE. And I'm asking you about the weeds –

CHRIS. – for help.

DEE. What with, love?

CHRIS. I said –

DEE. She's the one with the disease, you're not the one that needs help, love, really, are you?

CHRIS. Hm.

DEE. Now, get back up that hill and into that garden. I need a brew before this exam or I'll fall asleep while I'm invigilating – Oh, don't give me that look. Honestly, mountains and molehills, love. Just do the weeds, have a think and then pop up to Lewis Farm later on. Now, love, really, I have to get going, they're as strict about start times for these mock exams as they are for the real things –

CHRIS. But I've been in that church, trying to pray –

DEE. Oh, no –

CHRIS. – since the service, since Bea left, that's what? two? three hours? / Just asking for some guidance –

DEE. Love, your knees –

CHRIS. – She's barely spoken to either of us since we moved here, what twenty-five, thirty years ago? –

DEE. You just get like this sometimes –

CHRIS. – She just put the Bibles out – no, it's different – she asked me a question and what did I say? / Nothing, is what.

DEE. I've got to get this cuppa –

CHRIS. – I'm fine when it's raffles and an assembly or two, fine with the odd bit of pastoral care –

DEE. More than fine –

CHRIS. – but that question pushed through something that looked like stone and turned out to be rotten wood – / It's still echoing about inside me, unanswered –

DEE. You were caught off-guard, anyone would be –

CHRIS. Dee! Please.

> DEE *lets a short pause expose his brief loss of control and then indicates their surroundings.*

DEE. Playground, Chris.

CHRIS. Sorry, but… Mm.

> *A pause as* DEE *looks up at the sky, around the playground, anywhere but* CHRIS.

> CHRIS *goes to speak but* DEE *cuts him off.*

DEE. Why don't you defrost that joint? Leave it out tonight and we could have it tomorrow, nice bottle of red and a proper sit-down and a talk.

CHRIS. Tomorrow.

DEE. Well, I'll have all these exams to mark tonight –

CHRIS. Endless marking –

DEE. But tomorrow, we could have a talk while that thing's on telly, you know, the thing you like. Or if you want to just focus on that for a bit we could talk the day after, yeah?

CHRIS....

DEE. Do the weeds. Take your mind off it. Have a little think of what you'd like to say when you see her next and stay off those stone floors, for God's – Sorry, I mean, you know what I mean –

CHRIS. How long ago did we move here?

DEE. Love?

CHRIS. We were in our twenties, weren't we? Not so far away there are people wearing this collar in war zones, on national borders, cities.

DEE. Nicer here, though.

CHRIS. Safer. Easier, maybe.

DEE. Love –

CHRIS. Am I a coward? –

DEE. Ugh, Christ –

CHRIS. You've a gift for helping people. There's actual evidence of you helping people. Exam results and what-have-you, there's proof that you help people. You're the one making a difference, you're the one really impacting the future of humanity, / one child at a time.

DEE. Future of humanity?

CHRIS. I need your help –

DEE. The things Ida O'Connell posts online, love, if I'm impacting the future then / God help us.

CHRIS. I'm asking for your help cos I'm...

CHRIS *can't find the right word, a pause develops as he tries before he looks at* DEE, *helplessly.*

DEE. Soon. Okay, love? Soon.

4.

12:42 p.m.

DEE. It's a hoax, Ellen.

ELLEN. No, yeah, Miss, but –

DEE. 'Mrs', Ellen. Still, 'Mrs'.

ELLEN. Yeah, no, I know, but there have been all these sightings though –

DEE. 'All these sightings'?

ELLEN. No, yeah, Ida O'Connell's been saying she / saw one but –

DEE. Anyone other than the school... storyteller?

ELLEN. Yeah, no, loads, the Sterry twins say Naomi Kovac's brother told her that he was driving to town and saw one. And Manda Jenkins was saying that when she took her dog out for a walk it was scared. And Tom Vespa says the sheep are acting weird on the hill up there.

DEE. Ellen, love, 'the sheep are acting weird'?

ELLEN. Yeah, no, yeah, and Pete Musthill said –

DEE. Pete Musthill told me he saw one in the school hall so we can count him out.

ELLEN. No, yeah, yeah –

DEE. I'm asking for actual evidence, Ellen. Scientific evidence.

ELLEN. Yeah, no, but what if it was true though and we were all, like, all of us here in school, what if we were in danger though? They're 'apex predators', google it –

DEE. You want me to close the school.

ELLEN. Yeah, no, not me, but yeah.

DEE. You want me to close the school now. So, just before this afternoon's mock exam.

ELLEN. Yeah, no, no, but wolves are dangerous, though.

DEE. Ellen, you're a bright student. You're predicted good grades so far.

ELLEN. No, yeah, not that good –

DEE. They're good, Ellen.

ELLEN. Yeah, no, not good enough for, for getting into a good,
you know –

DEE. There are no wolves. Okay, love?

ELLEN. No, yeah, but you don't, like, know that.

DEE. I do.

ELLEN. Yeah, no, but –

DEE. It's a hoax. And not a clever one.

ELLEN. No, but –

DEE. You know those kids who hang about in the pub car park?
Well, they're not kids any more but you know, Kelly Mann,
Michael Button. You know them?

ELLEN. Yeah, no, I don't know them know them but I know
them –

DEE. Do you think this might be the kind of thing people like
those car-park kids might like to spread rumours about?
Create a bit of fuss, a bit of drama for a change, hey?

ELLEN. Yeah, no, someone released them. The wolves, bought
them online, released them.

DEE. Bought wolves online.

ELLEN. Yeah, no, it's not hard, it's like, a couple of grand,
I looked it up.

DEE. Did you.

ELLEN. Yeah, yeah, no, yeah, two grand tops.

DEE. You think they might have that kind of money, do you?

ELLEN. Yean, no, but Ida, her dad's this big, you know,
drug-dealer, yeah? So –

DEE. Did Ida say that too?

ELLEN. Yeah, no, but everyone knows it though, so –

DEE. Okay, love, so assuming Ida – an eleven-year-old in hand-me-downs – assuming she's got two thousand pounds spare. Assuming she can get a pack of wolves here, feed them, all of that. Why would she release them? And then be the first person to claim she saw one? And why here and not in the city or at an event or anything else?

ELLEN. No, yeah, yeah, no, but, maybe not Ida though.

DEE. Okay so why might *someone* do all of that?

ELLEN. Terrorism.

DEE. Terrorism.

ELLEN. Yeah, no, not usual terrorism, more like, a home-grown sort of thing. Someone who wants to like, disrupt our, you know, way of life. Someone who hates us because we've got like, freedom of speech and because they want what we've got and they're so backwards that they want to like, rewind the world and release wolves and make it like it was, like it all was with bears and that.

DEE. Right.

ELLEN. Yeah, no, you know, like forests and stuff. Maybe, like, they want, I don't know, get back to the beginning and start again or maybe it's just a farmer protesting about not getting government money – Maybe it's mad, old Bea Lewis –

DEE. I won't hear a word spoken against that woman. Specially not today.

ELLEN. No, yeah, no, but it might be someone who's just like mental, like Ida, she once covered herself in petrol and ran around setting fire to everything she touched – She did this, or said it anyway – And it's possible she got the wolves, Miss, so you should shut the school, because, if wolves got into the exam hall and, I mean, like how foxes are in hen houses, that'd be, you know, like, you'd be, like, responsible.

DEE. Ellen, do you think I'm a good teacher?

ELLEN. Miss? Mrs, I mean –

DEE. Am I a good teacher?

ELLEN. No, yeah, I mean. Yeah.

DEE. What is a good teacher, do you think?

ELLEN. Yeah, no, it's someone who... Who helps people by, um – Is this a test?

DEE. Helps people, how?

ELLEN. By, um, giving them feedback on how they're doing on things and helping them and... Why are we – ?

DEE. Give feedback...

ELLEN. Um, the wolves, I said about the –

DEE. You know Michael Button uploads videos? They're from a phone, I think you can hear Kelly Mann's voice in them, sometimes Ida's. She's got that stammer so... Have you seen them?

ELLEN. Why are you talking about – ?

DEE. I have. They're awful. I taught those kids. And the kind of people they've become. Or always were. Well, I didn't help them, did I?

ELLEN. I haven't seen them.

DEE. A lot of people have. A lot of views. Those kids, the ones with that emptiness inside them, I think that they might be even more dangerous than a pack of wolves.

ELLEN. Um... yeah, no, but, it's this place though, there's nothing to do, so –

DEE. I hear that so often –

ELLEN. No, yeah but –

DEE. You make things to do, it's called independence, love.

ELLEN. No, yeah, but people get stuck though and get boring and do all the same things and just become, you know, like nobodies.

Beat.

DEE. But you're not like those kids, are you? You're not like Michael Button or Kelly Mann. Ida O'Connell. Have I helped you? So far, I mean, have I helped you?

ELLEN. Yeah, no, no, yeah, you've yeah, you've helped me –

DEE. How?

ELLEN. You, um… nice. You're nice.

DEE. I'm nice.

ELLEN. Yeah, like, when… When people talk about my… weight. You said some nice things.

A pause develops – DEE *is looking at* ELLEN's *body and* ELLEN *is uncomfortable.*

DEE. Why do you think people get stuck?

ELLEN. Um, um –

DEE. Maybe cos people don't have the difficult conversations. The hard truths. Instead they *want* so much for some problems not to exist that they ignore even the most obvious. Do you think that might be true?

ELLEN. Yeah, no, um, yeah.

DEE. Because there are tough conversations, engaging the support systems that are in place for people like Kelly Mann, Michael Button, but maybe the tougher conversation is… does any of it ever work? Cos being 'nice' is just a way of not really getting involved, isn't it? Being 'nice' never impacted the future, did it? Not in a good way, I mean.

ELLEN. Yeah, no, Mrs Cobb, I actually wanted to –

DEE. Do you think being 'nice' would help Ida?

ELLEN *shrugs.*

Here's the truth, Ellen; you've a far better brain than those people. You don't need to avoid exams. Okay, love?

ELLEN. Yeah, no, I'm not though – I'm just –

DEE. It's Geography today, do you want to be a geographer?

ELLEN. Um –

DEE. Study nature? The impact of minor local changes on the planet as a whole – There's a fact about wolves actually, the knock-on effect of introducing them to an ecosystem, they can change everything. And geographers travel, do you want that?

ELLEN. Yeah, no, I, um –

DEE. What do you want to be? In your life, Ellen. Honestly, now. This isn't a test, imagine I'm your age, I'm your friend, we're lying on our backs on the school field, thinking about the future and I say, 'Hey, Ellen, what do you want to' –

ELLEN. Dancer.

DEE. A what? A dancer? What kind of dancer?

ELLEN. Doesn't matter.

DEE. Okay.

ELLEN. Just want to dance.

DEE. For a living?

ELLEN. Wanna dance to dance, to feel – Dancing, it's the only time I'm not, like, my name, my age, my grades, my suited career, a girl, ugly, fat, talked about – it's just here and now and alive and that's how I want to be, all the time, for ever –

DEE. You're built wrong to be a dancer. Being honest, Ellen. You'll never be a dancer.

ELLEN. Yeah, no, yeah, yeah, no, I'm, yeah, no, I'm…

5.

2:17 p.m.

ELLEN. What are you thinking?

FERDY *doesn't answer.*

What are you thinking, Ferdy?

Yeah, no, God, yeah, no, that's such a stupid thing to – I don't mean generally or – I just mean about what I just asked. What are you thinking, which way are you, you know, leaning?

Are you thinking about what I just asked? Or just busy with – with – with your stick or whatever. What are you doing with your stick?

Are you thinking like, good things? Like, sympathetic things? Like, 'Yeah, I'll help things' or... not?

Yeah, no, I mean it's a big thing to ask so don't, you know, give it some thought.

Bet you're thinking how come she's still here? How come she keeps coming down here when I barely say a word – You are quiet, aren't you? Old soul, that means. You are. Old soul.

Yeah, no, I mean, you're probably thinking, she's talking talking talking – It's all take take take with Ellen. Right? That what you're...?

I don't normally talk this much actually, my mum, she talks, Grace, you've probably heard of her, I think you've heard of her, she talks a lot, all the time. 'Ellen, you should be revising. Ellen, you need these results. Ellen, the world doesn't let people just get by, you don't want to end up a nobody, work hard, all the time, don't leave it to everyone else, you can't trust everyone else to do it the correct, you know, be on the council!' Just wants me to be her, just exactly the same as she is – Stupid woman, she's a total, you know... Grr!

Found a picture of her the other day from when she was my age, she wasn't always like that. Thinner than I am. Course. Not hard. Changes people, this place, she must have changed, must've become you know...

Yeah, no, yeah. Blah, blah, blah boring old Ellen.

Do you think I'm boring?

Think I'm a bit... think I'm gross? Sort of, repulsive and... '
Do I disgust you?

Am I disgusting to you?

Well, you're not so – You know, people say stuff about you
too, about your dreads, about how you never wash your hair
and you smell. And about the things you did in the war. And
about what you eat out here and benefits and – You're not,
like, not disgusting yourself, you know. You're like, people
say feral, people do actually say that. So... yeah.

Ex-SAS, they say. Ida O'Connell says anyway. So...
probably not true. Is it true?

Yeah, no, not my place, I'll just wait for you to, like, think it
over. I know it's like, I mean I guess it's illegal. Probably.
But it's something you can do, right?

Yeah, no, okay, as if you'd say, 'Yeah, I can do that for you,
Ellen, no problemo,' if it's illegal? You wouldn't, cos... And
just to be like, you know, what I mean by 'disappear' is
basically, like, I want you to just, make me, like *poof*! Just
gone. Not here, no trace, no chance of being found and
instead, I'm just, like... Elsewhere... The city, maybe or...
Can you do that?

Yeah, no, probably a lot of work in it, so yeah, think it over.
But I was thinking, I was supposed to be cramming for these
exams, for today's exam, the one that's happening now, but
there was this thing about how even tiny things affect the
whole planet, how all the terrible things we're doing, how
they're you know, making it worse for everyone everywhere
and it made me think about you and how you live and how
it's sort of, natural and... is that why? Are you trying to have
like, no effect or, less, you know, um...

But you're happy here, right? You're happy here. You
haven't got that constant feeling like you're angry all the
time, like, if you could you'd smash your bones to pieces
against every ancient idiotic wall and rule and thing and like

you're tired all the time and you're not hungry you can't be
hungry cos you eat but you've got this ache inside that won't
go away and you feel like if someone cut you you'd
probably not even bleed you're so... like you're just full
of... ash. Are you happy?

No, not my place to – Are you though?

Is it like, totally, like, what I'm asking is it totally mental to
you to hear me say that?

Cos I don't reckon it is, cos you live out here, right? You're
not, like, nowhere, but you're not – I mean – How do you
afford things? How do you ever pay for things?

Yeah, no, none of my – I'm not asking you to do it for free,
I've got money, it's a post office account, it's yours, you can
trust me, it's all yours, all my savings just, do it, yeah?

I've written the account details and the um, all the stuff,
here, it's... There. Okay, well, I'll leave it, oh, no, wet, so,
um... Here, yours. In your own time. But you'd better pick it
up before it gets, you know, like...

FERDY *stops and looks at the note that* ELLEN *has made*.

This is like a game I play with my dog. Curtis, he's a
Labrador, he's older than me but he's so good, you can put
biscuits on his nose and he won't take them. Not that you're
– I'm not saying you're – What's that smell? Is that? You
cooking something? Smells amazing. Stew or something?

FERDY *spits*.

Can you do it tonight? Or now, maybe? Cos, you know, the
wolves – Have you heard about this? You probably haven't
heard out here in the woods but the whole village is talking
about wolves, it's so stupid, it's so obviously just, like,
Michael Button or whatever, just like, winding people up but
everyone's so thick, they're totally buying it, so totally like
distracted –

Suddenly FERDY *looks at something somewhere in the
forest*.

ELLEN *tries to see whatever* FERDY *is looking at*.

What?

What was it?

FERDY *picks up* ELLEN*'s note and carefully tears it to pieces.*

NO! No, yeah? No. You help me. I've missed the exam, I'm not going back, not now, not with Mum, with – I'm not getting stuck here in this stupid, little village with these tiny little people – What's the point? You shouldn't be here either, you've *lived* and now you're just stuck here and it's just hiding, isn't it? Come on, Ferdy, take the money and – I'm the only one who visits, the only person you've got – We need this, both of us, we need to move on and – and – if you cared about me at all, you'd do this for me, and if not, if my own boyfriend won't even help me then –

FERDY. Boyfriend?

ELLEN. What? No, no, yeah, no, I mean, I don't, like, I mean –

FERDY. How old are you?

ELLEN. Nearly sixteen – Well, this time next year, I'll be nearly sixteen –

FERDY. Fourteen.

ELLEN. Yeah, no, no, but how does this affect any of it?

FERDY. You don't know me.

ELLEN. I just – I just want to – to leave –

FERDY. Go home.

ELLEN. No, I'm paying you to make me gone and I'm not leaving until –

FERDY *sniffs* ELLEN. *It's aggressive and invasive.* ELLEN *is shaken by it.*

FERDY. You stink.

ELLEN. What?

FERDY. I can smell it from here.

ELLEN. Stink?

FERDY. They smell it like sharks smell blood.

ELLEN. Who smells –

FERDY. Pack animals. They'll take your pets first. For betraying the pack. Then sniff out the weak.

ELLEN. Why are you saying this?

FERDY. Leave, now. Go on. GO!

6.

4:52 p.m.

FERDY. It's a stew.

GRACE. Is it?

FERDY. Venison stew.

GRACE. Oh?

FERDY. It's local. The meat. Locally caught. Not all venison. Some, other meat. I caught it all.

GRACE. Are you selling it?

FERDY. No. Giving it. Me to you.

GRACE. Can I get into my house, please?

FERDY. Yep.

GRACE. I just – I have to – Would you mind moving?

FERDY. You're Ellen's mum.

GRACE. You know my Ellen?

FERDY. Small town.

GRACE. Is she inside?

FERDY. Who?

GRACE. Ellen. Is Ellen inside?

FERDY. No.

GRACE. You don't... Do you know where she is?

FERDY. No.

GRACE. Sorry, I'm... Why are you bringing me a, er, a meat, um –

FERDY. There's some bird in it. Game, I mean.

GRACE. But, I'm asking 'why', Ferdy – It is Ferdy, isn't it?

FERDY. She comes to see me. Ellen. Your Ellen comes to see me sometimes.

GRACE. She...?

FERDY. Comes to see me. Talks.

GRACE. Ellen comes to your caravan? In the woods?

FERDY. Thought she wouldn't have told you, so. Stew.

GRACE. How long has this – ?

FERDY. A while. It's stopped now.

GRACE. Stopped?

FERDY. Yep.

GRACE. Okay, right, well, um, where is she?

FERDY *shrugs*.

By 'stopped', what do you mean? What do you mean 'it's stopped'?

FERDY. She got some bad ideas. Wrong ideas. She won't come back.

GRACE. What do – ? What do you mean she – ? Where is she?

FERDY. Left mine about an hour ago, longer.

GRACE. And that's when you...? When –

FERDY. I thought, I'll have a word with her mum. Bring the stew.

GRACE. Why? Why the stew? What's the stew about?

FERDY. Peace offering.

GRACE. 'Peace offering'? Why 'peace offering', what do you mean 'peace offering' – ?

FERDY. You've tried to have me moved on.

GRACE. Me?

FERDY. As I say, small town.

GRACE. No, not me, personally, you must know the council have to take petitions seriously – ?

FERDY. I don't need people to like me.

GRACE. Can you – Can you just – ?

GRACE *takes out her phone but as she starts to make a call, she's shaking and...*

FERDY. Just wanted to say, Ellen's got some wrong ideas. She has to be told, properly, not to not be who she is. Understood?

*...*GRACE *drops her phone.*

FERDY *goes to pick it up,* GRACE *panics a little.*

Screen's cracked.

GRACE. Can I have it, please?

FERDY. Yeah.

GRACE. Can you put it on the ground, the step, where you are and then go, um, further –

FERDY. Alright.

GRACE. Further back, can you go further back –

FERDY. Okay. Okay.

GRACE *fiddles with the phone.*

That looks broken.

GRACE. Stay there.

FERDY. You okay?

GRACE. I'm not scared.

FERDY. Alright –

GRACE. I'm not scared, this is my property, you're on my property, why should I be scared?

FERDY. I should go.

GRACE. Yes, yes you should, now, please.

FERDY. But I am good, me. Really.

GRACE. Me too. And Ellen. We're good, ordinary people, we shouldn't be – be made to feel –

FERDY. People make up stories about me.

GRACE. Well, okay –

FERDY. I'm a good person. People make things up.

GRACE. And that means they don't matter?

FERDY. Means they're not true.

GRACE. So? I want you to leave now, please, / thank you.

FERDY. Your daughter gets bullied.

GRACE. My daughter, you're telling me about my daughter, *you* feel you can tell *me* about the welfare of – of my daughter – I think I'd know if she were getting bullied at school –

FERDY. Not school. She needs a friend.

GRACE. I asked you to leave, I won't be – be – Now, please. Now.

7.

6:03 p.m.

GRACE. Well, don't just stand there –

HARRY. Right, mate, well –

GRACE. I'm reporting a crime, Harry.

HARRY. Okay –

GRACE. This isn't a friendly chat.

HARRY. I can tell –

GRACE. I was threatened, he was threatening me.

HARRY. The point is, mate –

GRACE. He stood here, where I am now, talking about Ellen. And now Ellen's not answering her phone, hasn't been home and school / finished three hours ago.

HARRY. Right, Grace, that's a pretty big claim –

GRACE. Do I have to spell it out, Harry? Do I have to spell out the crime that was committed?

HARRY. I've got threatening, um, antisocial –

GRACE. What else do you need to know?

HARRY. I've noted the complaint –

GRACE. It's not a complaint, it's a crime – I didn't call the police to *complain*.

HARRY. I've written it down, okay? I'm writing it down – / Just need a pen.

GRACE. What more do you need to make an arrest? At least as a precautionary measure –

HARRY. Arrest – ? Grace, it's a busy night, people are fretting about these wolf rumours –

GRACE. The rumours, they're… Oh, my – It was him!

HARRY. Say again, mate?

GRACE. He released the wolves.

HARRY. Who, Ferdy?

GRACE. There's your prime suspect. A loner, an environmentalist, a war veteran, someone with connections, violent connections, who isn't afraid of – of –

HARRY. The wolves are a joke, Grace –

GRACE. That's what it was about, he was talking about me trying to have him moved on, he was more or less telling me he'd released the wolves as some kind of act of retribution –

HARRY. There are no wolves, mate.

GRACE. Harry, this is about priorities. This is about the welfare of the community. Ferdy made his choice, he chose to live out there, to reject all of this, all of us, it's clear how he feels about us. The dreadlocks, the caravan, it means: 'I don't like your hair, I don't like your homes, I don't want to drink in your pub or come to your events.' He's living out there, syphoning off electricity – No, he is, Harry so don't give me that – Solar panels couldn't power the lights he's got – Who pays for that electricity? And how does he afford the diesel for that massive Land Rover of his? Is it even a legal Land Rover, the width of it? I'll tell you how he affords the diesel: benefits. We're paying for that – that monster in the woods – Does he pay any tax? Of course he doesn't, this is the disdain he's got for us, for our way of life – It's in his fundamental beliefs to be a parasitic animal, to not care – And someone like that doesn't respond well to threats, to the possibility of being moved on, someone like that, someone who knows violence –

HARRY. Alright, mate, calm down –

GRACE. – will respond with violence, it's all they know – It wasn't an accident that he knocked on my door, he chose me, the councillor, he chose me, to be frank, he chose to come to the head of this community, to give me the veiled threat of dead meat in a pot, Harry. 'Local meat', he called it. He doesn't belong here, Harry, he's a threat and he's your fault start to finish. Start with the root of the problem, arrest him as a suspect in the release of dangerous animals and see what he says under questioning, interrogate him, go on.

HARRY. Calm down, okay, / mate?

GRACE. I've said time and again there's no room in this village for him. It's an illegal dwelling! An unstable, illegal and temporary dwelling created by a person engaged in illegal activities. An illegal person! This is all because you've been so sure that we should be open to these people, talking about 'helping' Ferdy, as if he's not dangerous –

HARRY. He's a veteran –

GRACE. He's not a 'lest we forget', is he? He didn't march slowly towards the guns – He was a dropout before and he's unstable now, an unstable veteran, he knows weapons, who's to say he's not got weapons!? How else did he control those wolves?

HARRY. Okay, mate, look, it's most likely the car-park kids, you know, Ida O'Connell or something. There are no wolves.

GRACE. How do you know?

HARRY. How do I know – ?

GRACE. There aren't any wolves. How do you know that? Go on, prove there aren't any. Prove it. Prove Ferdy didn't release any wolves and put everyone's minds at rest. Go on.

HARRY. Mate. Come on –

GRACE. I'm not your 'mate', PC Jones. I'm asking you to do your job because my Ellen is missing. My Ellen. I've been calling / and calling –

HARRY. The phone signal around here is non-existent, she's a teenager, it's been less than three hours, mate –

GRACE. My daughter's missing!

HARRY. Officially, it has to be at least twenty-four hours or –

GRACE. You think it's a coincidence that he comes to me, tells me that she's been visiting him, threatens me with – with –

HARRY. His cooking –

GRACE. It's not funny, Harry, there are wolves, you can't deal with wolves, you're a village plod, you're a no one, get on the phone and get backup.

HARRY. '*Backup*'? Grace, this isn't telly –

GRACE. You need the dangerous animals unit out here, armed. Armed against wolves, against an armed person – These animals need terminating to protect my daughter – any of our children – You're not taking any of it seriously when we're this far away from being the prey of a dangerous, paranoid, loner, survivalist suffering from PTSD, who's releasing wild animals – Do you want this village to become another 'Pray For' hashtag on your watch? Do you want a piece of bloody art commemorating the death of a traditional British village at the hands of a lunatic who was known, IS KNOWN, to the authorities and took my daughter first –

HARRY. Grace, I'll take a drive down there, okay, mate? But forget about this wolf thing, there are no –

GRACE. You don't know that! You don't know that there definitely aren't any wolves, and my daughter has never been late home from school, never! We have a thing, a tea and cake thing, we've always had it, always, it's our thing, it's what we do and – and now you're refusing to search for her –

HARRY. Right, and tell me again, you got home and he had a pot –

GRACE. Of dead animals, animals that he'd killed – Oh, my God, oh my god – Test the meat! Have forensics test the meat, / find out what it is –

HARRY (*laughing*). Forensics? Grace, where do you think we are – ?

GRACE *screams*.

And then she controls and composes herself and tries to look nonchalant and powerful again.

GRACE. You're out of your depth. Her blood will be on your hands, Harry. Her blood on your hands.

HARRY. Leave it. Okay?

8.

8:13 p.m.

HARRY. Leave it just there, mate.

ANNA *is holding the corpse of an animal.*

ANNA. Okay. Sure. Right.

ANNA *doesn't put it down.*

I just, I couldn't leave it, you know? I was driving, it calms me down, usually – usually it calms me down to have a drive, specially when I'm visiting my mum – She's… difficult, you see, and ill and – I was only driving from up on the farm to the bypass, music on to calm me – You know, Springsteen and then it was just there. In the road. I didn't see it till too late and these roads are so narrow, I swerved, hit the hedge and now the car's back – back – up there – near the church, blocking the – Anyway, I think one wheel went over it but it didn't move or make a sound so maybe it was already… you know… And I know it's weird but I didn't want it to become a – a – one of those, like, road-death pancakes. Things that die shouldn't be just left so then I thought I'd just walk it down – Just walk it into – into – But there's no one about, I've never seen the village like this, it's not even that late but it's like there's a curfew or a dragon or something and – and then you pulled up, lights flashing and I was like, 'Oh, no, he's gonna think I'm mental or drunk and arrest me and I've got no ID' –

HARRY. Have you been drinking?

ANNA. No. No. A bit.

HARRY. You're not drunk, are you, mate?

ANNA. No.

HARRY. Right, cos the breathalyser's not working so I'm gonna have to take your word for it.

ANNA. No, I'm fine. Honestly. I just – Just a bit adrenalised from… everything.

HARRY. Do you want to put the dead dog down, mate?

ANNA. Yeah, yeah. Is it a dog?

She doesn't.

HARRY. Everyone's in the pub. That's why it all looks so abandoned. 'Blitz spirit' sort of a thing.

Gradually and carefully, HARRY *takes the dead animal from* ANNA.

Either the pub or line-dancing in the village hall. It's biweekly. Only time the place ever sees any action is line-dancing. It's good actually, you should try it some time. Instructor's a bit intense. Calls herself 'Emma-Lou'. Still, takes your mind off things.

ANNA. This isn't a wolf, is it? It's not a dead, um –

HARRY. It's a dog, it's gone a bit grey is all.

ANNA. A dog? A normal dog?

HARRY. Looks like Curtis to me.

ANNA. Curtis?

HARRY. Belonged to the Alberrys? Know them?

ANNA. Um, Grace Alberry?

HARRY. Yeah, and Ellen. Her daughter. Now, tell me again. He was just lying in the road?

ANNA. Yeah, yes, I was driving and, when I saw her, she didn't move at all, just the hand – the paw, it was like this, just trembling a bit, twitching –

HARRY. Old dog, deaf, probably didn't see or hear you coming.

ANNA. Just clipped her at most, she was just lying there –

HARRY. 'He', it's Curtis, so –

ANNA. Why was she out in the road like that? Who left her alone like that, when she's how old? In dog years? Eighty or something? It's irresponsible, that kind of thing – I mean unless she decided for herself, took herself off to die, I mean, do they do that? Dogs? Decide it's the end and just lie in the

– in the – Unless something killed it already and it was dead already, badger or fox, do they do that? Can they kill dogs?

HARRY *looks at the corpse closely. Pulls out some specs to help.*

What are you looking for?

HARRY. Just, ruling things out.

ANNA. But it's just hysteria, isn't it? This wolf stuff. Rumours and…

HARRY (*unconvincingly*). Yeah.

ANNA. There used to be a monster around here. My nan told me about it. 'Beast of Bodmin'-type thing, nonsense – I mean *her* nan had told her about it so I don't know how old this thing's supposed to be. But she *knew* it was still out here somewhere. Knew it. Waiting, watching. Cos my great-great-gran had been there when they'd chased it into the woods, it had took a baby or something, no one ever saw it but the whole village had come together. Lit the torches, grabbed the pitchforks, roaring, howling, roaming the forests like one big animal. The way Nan used to tell it, it sounded like it must have felt amazing, being in that mob, the torches, out all night together… But also makes you wonder if they were doing that, what if the villagers were really the beast all along. What really happened to that child. She was great at telling stories, Nana Lewis, all the stories are passed down by the women, maybe cos they tell the children, talk more, live longer…

A sound somewhere not so far away draws their attention for a moment.

Should we maybe get in your car? Go inside somewhere? I need to call my mother, anyway, she's alone up on the hill and –

HARRY *looks around a bit, trying to look tough but clearly a little shaken.*

HARRY. Yeah, I know your mum.

ANNA. You know her?

HARRY. Harry. Harry Jones. From the little house near the –

ANNA. Harry!?

HARRY. Yeah. Yes.

ANNA. Wow.

HARRY. I know.

ANNA. You've changed, you've really – Maybe it's the uniform – Suits you! It's been, how long?

HARRY. I know.

ANNA. You had a kid, didn't you? You had a baby with, what was her name? Malarkey –

HARRY. Rosie.

ANNA. Rosie Malarkey! Yes, lived up to that name, didn't she? She got me drunk in the churchyard, cheap cider, I still can't stand it! How is she? How's… Oh, sh-ugar.

HARRY. It's okay.

ANNA. I completely forgot.

HARRY. It's fine.

ANNA. I'm sorry. It was recent, wasn't it?

HARRY. Sort of, sort of not, mate – I'm not gonna bore you with this, though.

ANNA. We were friends.

HARRY. Yeah. Long time ago.

ANNA. Hey, if everyone's in the pub maybe we should… Well, we could go and join? Catch up a bit? I mean, I know you're working, but… Christ! I just, I'd like to go for a drink is all. With you.

A little pause develops as HARRY *and* ANNA *lock eyes.*

Eventually, HARRY *looks away.*

HARRY. Can't.

ANNA. Right.

HARRY *is clearly, very nervous.*

Are you okay?

HARRY. Yeah, mate, course.

ANNA. It's just... you looked at me then, like I'm some kind of a threat.

HARRY. Something killed the dog. And there's a young girl missing, Ellen's missing, so...

ANNA. You don't seriously think...

HARRY. I don't know, you see.

ANNA. Right. Right. Okay. Right.

The sound of howling echoes out across the village.

ONE. The sound of howling rolls around the shallow valley and in through the windows of Grace's double-locked house, interrupting her phone call.

GRACE (*gradually losing interest in her phone call*). No, I know it's only been five hours but our local policeman is a disast... er...

ONE. The sound rolls through the pub garden to where Ferdy stands, like this.

TWO. He's been watching the people inside through the windows, feeling a familiar ache, an ache that – at the same moment he hears the howling – he can finally name, he's feeling –

FERDY. Lonely. Bit too lonely.

ONE. Recklessly, against his better judgement and for the first time in who knows how long, Ferdy decides to be brave, to try to join in, to go into the pub.

TWO. Further up the hill, the howling dies against Dee's headphones. She should be marking geography exams. Instead, she's online watching videos uploaded by ex-pupils. Bullying videos. Cruel videos.

DEE (*disturbed*). Oh, Ida, love... Ida... Ida... Ida.

TWO. The howls pass into the living room where her husband, the vicar, is watching a nature documentary.

ONE. Chris didn't do the weeding earlier. He looked at it for a long time before saying...

CHRIS. Hm.

ONE. And now, muting the documentary to check where the howling is coming from, he says...

CHRIS....hm.

TWO. Up at the brow of the hill, on Lewis Farm, the howling brings the tremble back into Bea's hand. She stops rolling out the extra barbed wire and has two thoughts...

BEA. Quad bike. Shotgun and quad bike.

TWO. Even Ellen hears the howling, though no one knows where she is.

ONE. But back in the middle of the road, with the sun dipping behind the brow of the hill on the other side of the shallow valley, the mist starting to pool as night draws in, with everything looking just how it must have looked when all this was truly, properly, wild... Anna says –

ANNA. Doesn't sound like kids to me.

HARRY. Anna, mate, mind going to the pub for me? Let them know there'll be a muster point in the village hall. Need everyone there.

ANNA. Sure, okay, fine, um, is that – is this what you're supposed to do in this kind of situation?

HARRY (*afraid*). I don't know, mate.

TWO. We're going to pause there for a little while to have a cup of tea and a break. Thanks for your help so far.

End of Act One.

Interval

During the interval, the performers mingle with the audience.

They might answer questions about the play and could ask questions about this particular location.

As the interval draws to a close, they return to the playing space.

ACT TWO

[NOTE: Perhaps a useful rule for clarity in this challenging second act, is that whenever ONE *or* TWO *discuss or describe a character, the character being described or discussed is played by the relevant actor, making them visible.]*

ONE. Are we all here? Everyone ready?

Maybe there's a response, maybe not.

ONE *and* TWO *might engage in a little ad lib about the raffle or somesuch, always including the audience, always welcoming, always conjuring a sense of community and joy.*

Okay, so, we left Anna Lewis, stood in the road with PC Harry Jones, and the body of the dead dog. Howling echoing around them.

ANNA. Sure, okay, fine, um, is that – is this what you're supposed to do in this kind of situation?

HARRY (*afraid*). I don't know, mate.

TWO. Not far away, as the sun dips behind our hill, Ferdy braves the excitable, busy pub for the first time in who knows how long to order a –

FERDY. Pint of… whatever people normally get, please.

TWO. Stars brighten, mist pools in the shallow valley, night gathering around the church, the rectory, Dee can't hear the howling, she's wearing headphones, watching online videos –

DEE (*disturbed*). Oh, Ida, love… Ida… Ida… Ida.

TWO. But Chris heard it.

ONE. Chris, the vicar, has turned off his nature documentary to answer the phone. It's Harry. Harry's telling him about the roll-call that's about to happen in the village hall.

CHRIS. Hm.

ONE. Harry's asking him to come quickly. Asking him not to panic. Asking him to hurry but calmly.

CHRIS....Hm.

TWO. And Bea, in spite of her still-trembling hand, loads her gun, repeating –

BEA. My lambs, my lambs, my lambs, my lambs –

ONE. Soon, Grace is on her way to the village hall, carrying tins of muffins that she's compulsively baked since her encounter with Ferdy. Still no sign of Ellen.

TWO. No one knows where Ellen is. Not even us. But inside the village hall, which was built on the Norse church, on the Roman church, on the pagan church, where the fires used to be...

ONE *cues line-dancing music. Maybe 'Boot Scootin' Boogie'.*

EMMA-LOU (*bad American accent*). And five, six, five six seven eight!

(*Talks through the steps, for example:*) Left.

Right.

Left, right, left, heel.

Heel.

Step, kick, heel, kick.

TWO. Emma-Lou. Real name Sharon. And the rest of the line-dancers didn't hear the howling over their music.

EMMA-LOU (*jolly*). Pope!

POPE (*getting the steps wrong*). Hey!?

EMMA-LOU. You're out of step there, cowboy, we're on the left, still the left.

POPE (*wrong*). What? Left?

EMMA-LOU (*American accent falters into a broad regional accent*). Back to the right, Pope!

POPE (*even more wrong*). I'm loving this!

ONE. Besides Pope, there's Mr King.

KING. Alright?

ONE. He's a local battery farmer though he prefers to call it –

KING. Intensive farming.

ONE. It's caused a bit of friction in the village, few cold
shoulders, probably more in his own head than in reality but
here, he gets to fall in line, escape himself a bit, feel a little –

KING. Yee-haw, Emma-Lou?

EMMA-LOU (*American. Jolly*). Yee-haw, Mr King!

(*Tense*.) Pope – POPE!

POPE. Huh?

EMMA-LOU (*American, jolly*). We're stepping, we're
stepping –

POPE. What!?

EMMA-LOU (*broad, angry*). STEPPING! POPE, STEPPING!

(*American, jolly*.) Okay, guys, good goin'.

TWO. Then there's Mel. This is her biweekly night of not
having to do bed and bathtime.

MEL. Hahaha-this-is-great-isn't-it-great-it's-great.

TWO. The mechanical act of simply following steps lets her
forget for moments at a time the myriad responsibilities of
parenting toddlers.

MEL. I-am-having-the-BEST-time. (*Checks her watch*.)

EMMA-LOU (*American*). Nice job, Mel. Really working that
cowboy –

(*Faltering*.) Not to the right, Pope –

POPE (*delighted*). Right? Right, am I?

EMMA-LOU. No, to the – Forget it. Great job there, Mr King.
Rootin' tootin' Injun shootin'!

KING. Alright.

MEL. Yeah-I'm-alright-more-than-alright-I'm-yee-haw-you-know-Injuns!

EMMA-LOU. From the top again!

(Talks through the steps, for example:) Left.

Right.

POPE. Right again?

EMMA-LOU. Left now – LEFT, Pope, LEFT, heel.

Step, kick, heel, kick.

KING. Alright!!

EMMA-LOU. Yeehaw! And, left, right, left...

TWO *begins to dance differently, more tribal, more angry, to a different beat.*

EMMA-LOU *gradually noticing, patience faltering before addressing her.*

You're getting it wrong there, babycakes, just gotta take 'er a lil easier.

Listen to the rhythm, cowgirl, you're not...

By now TWO *is dancing as* ELLEN.

Okay, if you wanna dance like that you, book the hall out yourself, love. Yeah?

Can you hear – Hello?

For a moment the music switches into the music inside ELLEN*'s head. Maybe Skrillex's 'Bangarang'.*

EMMA-LOU *keeps line-dancing whilst watching* ELLEN *dancing a dance of frustration and anger.*

EMMA-LOU *waves at* ELLEN *and says something that we cannot hear over the music.* ELLEN *doesn't notice.*

EMMA-LOU *eventually taps* ELLEN *on the shoulder.* ELLEN *stops. So does her music. Instead, we hear the line-dancing music again.*

(Broad.) Do you mind? It's booked, this place. By me.

ELLEN *leaves*.

(*American, jolly*.) Okay, cowboys! Keep it moving – Whooo-hooo!

EMMA-LOU*'s whoop becomes a howl*.

The howl reverberates momentarily before –

HARRY. Sorry, mate. Right. Most of you know but, health and safety, I'm PC Jones, you can still call me Harry. I'm sorry to interrupt but we've got a precautionary thing happening. Protocol. It's a roll-call for your safety and security. Fellas from the pub, in you come. This hall is now an official muster point, just making sure no one's missing. Now… anyone got a pen?

Maybe someone has. Maybe not. HARRY *finds one somehow*.

Right. 10 p.m. Is the vicar here?… no?

This slightly knocks HARRY *but he tries to push through it*.

Okay, well, in no particular order then. So, bit of calm, bit of quiet. Just say 'here', loud as you can, if you hear your name. Okay?

[*Name of audience member.*]

[*Name of audience member.*]

[*Name of audience member.*]

Ferdy?

FERDY *flinches*.

Saw you coming in from the pub – Lewis, Anna. Anna Lewis.

ANNA. Yes, I mean, here, sorry.

HARRY. And Bea Lewis? Did you get hold of your mum or – ?

ANNA. I haven't got any signal, has anyone got any signal? Or a car / I could borrow to just –

HARRY. It's okay, mate, this is what roll-calls are for.

ANNA. It's just she's not as capable as she thinks she is –

HARRY. We'll collect all the names, mate, then work out what needs to be done. (*Writing*.) Bea Lewis... not here.

GRACE *fidgets nearby*.

Yeah, Grace, mate, already know about Ellen –

GRACE. But could you please tell us what's going on here?

HARRY. It's a precaution for your safety and security.

GRACE. So there is a threat.

HARRY. Yeah, well, that's what's being avoided so –

GRACE. We all heard the howling, my –

HARRY. Yeah and –

GRACE. – daughter's missing and I've just found out that my dog's been killed –

HARRY. Well, not necessarily –

GRACE. I think I deserve – I think we all deserve to know what's happening here.

HARRY. Yeah, mate, if I can just –

GRACE. But what is it – Is it wolves? Is it some individual, some group or – or –

HARRY. Grace, calm, yeah, just –

GRACE. We just want to know why we're being kept here, why *you* are in here, instead of looking –

The doors of the village hall slam.

HARRY. That better have been someone coming in. Everyone knows not to leave, right? I did say that – Where's Anna?

TWO. Anna's already across the car park, running, running towards the farm at the top of the hill. Every breath, panting the word 'Mum, Mum, Mum' –

HARRY. Christ, right. No one leaves, okay? Police orders – [*name of FOH or village-hall manager*], lock the doors for us, mate.

GRACE. We're not allowed to leave?

HARRY. And give us the keys after, yeah – [*name of FOH or village-hall manager*]?

GRACE. People are missing here.

HARRY. I just need everyone to keep calm and to –

GRACE. People are missing here. The vicar, his wife, the Lewises, my daughter, they're all out there with God knows what, God knows who, and your plan is to lock the doors?

HARRY. It's the first stage of the plan, mate –

GRACE. What's the second stage?

HARRY. It comes after the roll-call so if I can just –

GRACE. What's the second stage of your plan?

HARRY. Grace. I'm a police officer.

GRACE. Tell me, what's the second stage?

HARRY. It's... find out who's missing.

GRACE. That's the first stage, you just said that's the first stage. What's the second stage?

Hopefully FOH or village-hall manager has delivered the keys by now and been thanked.

HARRY. Wait for help. [*If necessary:*] Where are those keys, mate?

GRACE. Wait. In here? In this fortress – How safe do you think this place is?

HARRY. It's safe, it's... it's a safe –

GRACE. These dogs, they killed Curtis – They hunt at night, they'll take the oldest and youngest first –

HARRY. Grace, mate, it's not likely it's wolves, is it?

GRACE. Worse then. Someone's out there, hunting our pets, children –

HARRY. No, mate –

GRACE. We know the stories, attacks like this do happen, in small communities with hunting, farming, weapons, the loners, outsiders, we know this, don't we? We do.

HARRY. Now, don't start –

GRACE. 'Don't start' what!? Responding? There are people missing and you're here doing what?

HARRY. Well, normally the vicar would do this bit so I could take the car but –

GRACE. But she's out there, in danger?

HARRY. Yeah, let me finish and then –

GRACE. You can't do this alone, you know that, don't you? Have you called for support?

HARRY....

GRACE. Have you called for support, PC Jones?

HARRY. The landline's been disconnected.

GRACE. The landline in the hall? Here? You only tried to call for support from here? What about your radio?

HARRY. Just… Um, Stacey O'Connell? She here?

GRACE. I asked about your radio.

HARRY (*quiet*). Not working.

GRACE. Couldn't hear that.

HARRY. It's not working.

GRACE. Your radio's not – ! His radio's not working. Why isn't your radio working?

HARRY. Stacey, is Ida here?

GRACE. Whose phone is working? Anyone got any coverage? We need the dangerous animals unit. / Start calling or texting people you know, just anything you can to –

HARRY. No, I'm doing names, mate. Everyone – EVERYONE!

A smash comes from off – GRACE *and* HARRY *are terrified.*

Everyone is frozen for a moment, gripped with fear.

GRACE. It came from the toilets.

HARRY....

GRACE. Well?

HARRY. Yeah, yeah. Um...

GRACE. Are we even going to have to check in there for ourselves?

HARRY. ...here's your pen back, mate.

GRACE. I told you they were out there, that they'd come for us –

HARRY. Alright –

GRACE. No, it's not alright, we're relying on you to –

HARRY (*losing it*). ALRIGHT, MATE! Alright... I'll... yeah.

HARRY *tries to steel himself and head towards the toilets.*

DEE. I told you to bring a torch, didn't I, love? Didn't I say, 'Bring a torch'?

CHRIS. Hm.

DEE. I said, 'Bring a torch, Chris, so we can see where we're going.'

CHRIS. Let's go back and get the car.

DEE. No.

CHRIS. Harry needs me at the village hall.

DEE. Well...

CHRIS. Well what?

DEE. I said I wanted to walk.

CHRIS. But you were watching videos online.

DEE. You were watching telly.

CHRIS. So, Dee, why – ?

DEE. Do we still love each other or is this just easier?

CHRIS *stops for a moment before...*

CHRIS. Hm.

DEE. You were saying all that about me being good at helping people, I'm not. I'm good at being nice, at enabling, but I can't help people. It's how I've been about us, not rocked the boat, left us to drift and drift. And now I'm bored, I'm so bored. And you are too, I know you are, we're filling time, talking about the next meal, that's all. And I'm not helping my students, they're time bombs, some of them, Ida today, she'd a look in her eye that was... It's genuinely how I think murderers might look and I don't know how this has all happened, I don't understand these kids, can't talk to them and all the time, inside, I'm their age, I'm more like – [*the age that* ONE *feels inside*] on the inside, not saggy and old and hairy under my arms, inside I'm – [*the age that* ONE *feels inside*] and my hair's still – [*describes* ONE*'s own hair as it was when she was that age*]. But I'm not, am I? Somehow, when we weren't looking, we lost touch, we got boring and all I've been able to think about since you came to the school on morning break is that if I thought I was turning into a wild animal, if I was Bea Lewis, I would run. So far. For so very, very long. Because I am bored. We're bored. Both of us. And maybe we just need to say it. You know, love, to... to have the talk.

CHRIS. Hm.

A pause develops.

DEE. What's your face doing? It's too dark, love. I can't see your face. What's it doing?

CHRIS. Um –

DEE. Does this mean anything to you at all or...?

CHRIS. Mm.

DEE. Ugh, that bloody sound –

CHRIS. Music.

DEE. ...what?

CHRIS. Is that a car up ahead?

We can hear 'Dancing in the Dark' playing in the distance.

DEE. Did you hear anything I just said –

CHRIS. Whose car is it?

DEE. I don't –

CHRIS. Why would someone leave their car like this, here? No room for anyone to get past. Are the windows intact?

DEE. I don't – HELLO!? Anyone –

CHRIS. There wouldn't be a muster if there weren't some kind of danger out here, would there?

DEE. Danger? Really, you think there's –

CHRIS. It's unlocked.

DEE. What are you doing?

The music stops.

CHRIS. Saving the battery.

CHRIS *suddenly thinks he sees something.*

DEE. Christopher.

CHRIS. Hm.

DEE. Chris.

CHRIS *looks the other way, certain now.*

Stop acting like a bloody child.

CHRIS. Something's out there, / I can hear running.

DEE. Don't be / silly.

CHRIS. I'm not being silly, I'm / being serious.

DEE. You're just / trying to –

CHRIS. Get in.

DEE. What?

CHRIS. Get in the car.

DEE. I don't know who's it is, / I'm not about to –

CHRIS. In, now!

Car doors slam and reverberate into a shattering sound.

TWO. Back in the village hall, just after the window in the toilets smashed, Harry is creeping into the village loos with nothing but his self-defence training to protect him from...

TWO *notices some pain in her hand.*

...from whatever might have broken in.

TWO *bursts a small blood pack and begins to act the pain that IDA feels.*

HARRY. It's alright! Alright, everyone. Coast's clear...

Inside the locked toilet cubicle, IDA is bleeding but trying not to. She whimpers a little in pain but holds it in.

HARRY *listens carefully, animal-like.*

IDA *tries to stop breathing.*

HARRY *pretends to walk away.*

IDA *whimpers a little more freely.*

Right, who's in there?

IDA....

HARRY. Come on. Out. Now.

IDA....

HARRY. I know you're in there, mate, out you come and stop sneaking about.

IDA. Ss – Sss – Not ss – ss –

HARRY. Ida?

IDA. Not sss-neaking –

HARRY. Ida O'Connell. Mate, what have I said about this kind of thing?

IDA....

HARRY. You know pretty much the whole village is out there? You know they all thought you were a wolf, hey? They already blame you for smashing all the pubs windows that night –

IDA. No –

HARRY. – and half of them reckon it was you started that fire in the school. / Now's not the time to be mucking about.

IDA. No. Not me. Didn't do them things.

HARRY. What happened in here? Did you smash that window?

IDA....

HARRY. You know your mum's in the other room. Want me to send her in to get you? –

IDA. Sss-she been drinking? –

HARRY. Both your brothers are out there too, could send them all in here. Want me to go and get them? Set them on you? –

IDA. Don't care –

HARRY. – Cos honestly, mate, I'm sick of this, I've got my hands full in there, last thing I need is you kicking off – Just, come on, mate. Out.

IDA....

HARRY. NOW!

HARRY is suddenly worried about raising his voice in earshot of the village hall.

Was it you? Hey? All this? Starting rumours? Playing tricks? –

IDA. Didn't make it up –

HARRY. – Is that why you smashed this window, is it? To keep winding people up, keep scaring people?

IDA. No.

HARRY. Did you break this window?

IDA....yeah.

HARRY. And you told everyone you saw a wolf, that's what they're all saying –

IDA. Cos I did ss – ss-see a wolf. In the woods. On my way to ss-/ssschool.

HARRY. Right, I'm not having this conversation through a
   bloody door! Open it now or I'll… Why did you break the
   window for?

IDA.…

HARRY. Huh? Why did you / break it?

IDA. Not ss-saying.

HARRY. Not – GAH! How many times have we ended up
   having to have a little chat, hey? Always ends up being you –
   You know I could smash this down, don't you?

IDA. Go on then.

   HARRY *paces, kicking some of the broken glass into the
   corners with his feet as he goes.*

HARRY. Look, this is… The whole village is out there terrified.
   I need you to just come out to put them all at ease, okay?
   Come on, mate. I'm a police officer not a bloody foster parent.

IDA. No.

HARRY (*quiet*). I'll give you a fiver.

IDA. No.

HARRY (*quiet*). Tenner, then. I'll give you a tenner, just –

IDA. Not coming out.

HARRY. Right. (*Checking.*) I've got, I've got about twelve
   quid, twelve twenty-three, come on.

IDA. Not till you sss-say sss-sorry.

HARRY. Till I what? Till I –

IDA (*deep breath*). Say ss-sorry.

   HARRY *pretend smashes the door and silent screams before
   calming down.*

HARRY. What do I need to say 'sorry' about, mate?

IDA. I didn't lie.

HARRY. But you smashed a window to keep stirring / the
   whole thing –

IDA. No. To get out.

HARRY. Out? What's wrong with the doors, if you want to get out?

IDA. Locked.

HARRY. Why did you want to get out?

IDA. Kill one.

HARRY. To what? Kill one? You know that's a bit psycho, don't you? You know that's a bit – you know – I mean, why? Why did you want to kill a wolf, wear its skin to school or something?

IDA. Wanted to help –

HARRY. Help? Help who?

IDA. You.

HARRY is suddenly and unexpectedly moved.

HARRY. Mate, what makes you think I need any –

IDA. They've got packs. Wolves. You haven't. Sss-so thought I'd help.

A pause develops. HARRY sits on the floor.

PC Jones?

HARRY. Yeah, yeah, I'm still here.

IDA. No one else there, is there?

HARRY. No, mate.

IDA is still trying to conceal the pain of the cut on her hand but whimpers a little.

What was that, mate?

IDA. Nothing.

HARRY. You okay in there?

IDA. Yeah.

HARRY. Mate, you know you're eleven years old, don't you?

IDA. Course I do!

HARRY. Alright –

IDA. Not sss-stupid, am I?

HARRY. Alright, alright, just… How were you gonna kill a
wolf, then? Hey?

IDA. Trick it.

HARRY. Right.

IDA. Trick it ss-so it'd truss – ss – me and then kill it when it
was happy.

HARRY. And then what?

IDA. Sss-show everyone sss-o they wouldn't hate me any more.

HARRY. Who said they hate you, mate?

IDA. Most people, online mostly, ss-ssome to my face –

HARRY. Yeah, well, what it is, right? Is you've done some
things. And, people… Life's hard, you know? So, people,
they need to make their minds up quickly about stuff. But,
when it comes to real things. The village, the whole village,
it's bigger than those little, you know, quick decisions cos…
you know… there used to be a beast lived around here. Long
time ago. Beast lived out in the woods and the whole village,
yeah? It got everyone together, pitchforks and flaming
torches and that, they went out and they… got it.

IDA. Killed it?

HARRY. Yeah, they –

IDA. How?

HARRY. Um, well, they –

IDA. Got it and put it in a bin and some lighter fluid and set fire
to it and cut its head off with a penknife.

HARRY. Dunno the ins and outs, mate – The thing is, it took
everyone to get the beast. Yeah? And when it comes down to
it, the village isn't everyone without you. Is it? And we need
everyone if we're gonna kill a wolf, don't we?

IDA....

HARRY. What I'm saying is, you've gotta give 'em a chance to change their minds. You know? A village isn't just the people in it, is it? All the different people who've been there before, all their stories and... and you're one of them. You're a talking point. You're a story. So you can decide what happens next or how it ends –

IDA. By killing –

HARRY. No, just... Thanks for wanting to help me.

IDA. You're just trying to get me out.

HARRY. No. I'm not. Well, I am but... What I'm saying is you do stupid stuff but you've a good heart.

IDA. But everyone always thinks I'm lying.

HARRY. Well, you do lie sometimes, don't you?

IDA. Not about the wolf, I sss-saw that, I did.

HARRY. But you do lie sometimes and it confuses people. Me too, if I'm honest.

IDA. Not lying.

HARRY. No?

IDA. No.

HARRY. What would you call it then? If you're saying something's happened when it hasn't happened? Changing the truth? / Changing facts –

IDA. Sss-sstories.

HARRY. Stories, right. Overactive imagination, is it?

IDA. Sss-sometimes there's things you don't want to be true. And things you want to be better.

HARRY. Yeah, well, that's what I'm saying, mate. Means it's hard for people to trust you if you're... fibbing, doesn't it?

IDA....

HARRY. Now, are you gonna come out?

IDA. No.

HARRY. Right. Just want to stay in there, do you?

IDA. Yeah.

HARRY. Stay in there and avoid everyone who's angry with you, that it?

IDA. Don't get my mum.

HARRY. Okay –

IDA. Don't get her.

HARRY. Alright –

IDA. Don't though. Or my brothers.

HARRY. Fine, mate, I won't.

IDA. And don't tell her I'm in here.

HARRY. Okay, okay. But she needs to know you're safe, so –

IDA. Doesn't.

HARRY. Right, well, I won't tell them. I'll just… I'll make something up.

IDA. Bird hit it.

HARRY. Well –

IDA. Bird hit the window.

HARRY. I might not say that but –

IDA. It did, bird hit it and smashed through it and died cos it was trapped in here and wanted to get out but it died. That's why there's blood.

HARRY *touches the floor and looks at his finger, maybe he just found a spot of blood? Could the bird story be true?*

HARRY. I tell you what, it's very brave, what you wanted to do. Your idea.

IDA. Killing one?

HARRY. Yeah, it's the kind of idea that only comes to very brave people. And the brave thing to do, for both of us, yeah? Is to go back into that hall together, so –

IDA. You haven't sss-said 'sorry' yet for thinking I made up the wolf.

Having tried to stop the bleeding, IDA*'s hands are a bit messy with her own blood.*

HARRY. So what am I gonna tell them? That Ida's in the loos, she was trying to get out and what happened?

IDA. Ss-smass –

HARRY. Right.

IDA. Ssss –

HARRY. Okay.

IDA. You have to let me do the word or it won't get better.

HARRY. Sorry, mate.

IDA. Sss-sss – (*Deep breath.*) smashed glass. Fell on me.

HARRY. Yeah.

IDA. ...no.

HARRY. Not lying?

IDA. No!

HARRY. Not telling stories – ?

They hear the howling of wolves.

The howling warps, filling with the sound of panic from the village hall before becoming...

IDA. HAH! Hear that? Hearing that? That's wolves, that is, hear it?

HARRY. Yep.

IDA. Ss-see now!?

HARRY. Yep, okay. I'm sorry. Yeah? Sorry, Ida.

...the sound of an engine, howling, roaring and screeching through mud.

ONE. But before that, before Harry found Ida, before any of that, Anna was crashing through the woods, headed for her mother's farm. Lungs bursting, everything hurting, as she chased the sound and lights of the –

ANNA. STOP!

(*Trying to recover her breath.*) Stop.

Mum...

Christ. Think I might be...

Gonna be sick...

BEA. Vicar?

ANNA. Hey?

BEA. Why's it happening, Vicar?

ANNA. No, it's me, Mum. Your daughter, it's Anna –

BEA. No, no, I know you. You work for the council. Grace, isn't it? Alberry, kept your husband's name even after he left you.

ANNA. No, Mum, / you've been out all day –

BEA. Spoiled that chubby little daughter of yours, desperate – and now what? Want rid of my farm? Want more of those new-builds, hey?

ANNA. You're just tired –

BEA. Tired?

ANNA. It's late or early, we're all tired, now come with me, we have to get to the village hall.

BEA. You're him... from the dance.

ANNA. Sorry?

BEA. You're the man from the dance. The End of the World Dance, it was called.

ANNA. No, that was Dad –

BEA. Hall, you said –

ANNA. Yeah, but that dance was a long time ago.

BEA. They've always danced in that hall, from before there was a hall.

BEA *begins to sway, not so much dancing as something a little more animal.*

ANNA. Okay, Mum, you're not making any sense.

BEA. You always danced, even on your own –

ANNA. No, not me, Mum –

BEA. – the story of who you are or were, your body, music, people.

ANNA. No, no, / you're just confused.

BEA. You know you look just like him.

ANNA. This is it, you know that? This is what it does – No, stop, Mum, come on, stop that.

BEA *growls at* ANNA *who instinctively retreats from* BEA.

Yeah, very funny. Now, we have to go to the hall, there's a girl missing, there are bad things out here, the police are involved so now's not the time to be running about with a bloody shotgun – Just, come on!

BEA *begins to growl more and more aggressively.*

Oh, great, very grown up. When the police get here and they've heard about a threat in the woods and see a mad old lady with a gun –

BEA *begins to leave.*

Mum! Are you – Wait, no, I didn't mean *you're* mad, I meant it like a saying, like 'mad old – '

ANNA *grabs* BEA*'s hand but* BEA *bites at* ANNA, *frightening her a bit.*

It happens, Mum. People get old. No matter how difficult
you want to be about it. If it isn't this that kills you, it'll be
something –

BEA *mixes sniffs and barks into the growling – all directed
at* ANNA.

I'm on your side, I am on your side with all of this, of course
I bloody am but look at us! Middle of nowhere, in danger,
because you're too bloody stubborn –

BEA *begins to howl louder and louder.*

Just could sell the farm! It could pay for the best surgeons or
ANYTHING but don't just sit here with your bloody lambs
and no one – Mum, I just want you to bloody – Fine! FINE!

ANNA *howls with* BEA.

ANNA *out-howls* BEA.

BEA *watches her until* ANNA *stops, breathless and teary.*

You're impossible.

BEA. So are you.

ANNA. Is this about me not wanting the farm? Because I thought
we'd had that one years ago –

BEA. It's not about that –

ANNA. – I get that it's the end of the line, no more Lewises,
Nan used to talk about that all the time –

BEA. She was wrong.

ANNA. Wrong? Nan was wrong. What was she wrong about?

BEA. More non-Lewises than Lewises made that farm.
Marriages, people who've worked it, it's a mongrel farm.
The only pure thing's the work, doesn't matter who does it.

Somewhere in the distance a police siren.

ANNA. If you want to go mad and die out here, I just need to
know that it's your own, clear-minded, choice. Not you
making a point or... I just want you to be happy.

BEA. I am.

ANNA. But will you be? Until... until someone finds your little...

ANNA *surprises herself by being unexpectedly moved as she completes this sentence.*

...body?

ANNA *controls herself again.*

Will you be happy?

BEA *looks up and around her.*

BEA *smiles then, at* ANNA *as if this is answer enough.*

What does that mean? What was that? What did that mean?

BEA *shrugs.*

BEA. I'm hungry.

ANNA *makes a kind of whimper of inarticulate frustration.*

You should have a go with the gun. Helps.

GRACE. Lights, we need lights. The amdram club bought some theatre lights, par cans, they're called, aim them at the car park, the woods, see who's doing this – Or use them as a signal! Signal anyone who's out there that we're in here and – and –

HARRY. Mate, those lights –

GRACE. Harry, you're out of your depth – You didn't even find out what happened to the window!

HARRY. Well, it's safe so –

GRACE. We'll handle this.

HARRY. But running par cans off this circuit –

GRACE. We need the keys. The keys to the big cupboard at the back. Now, Harry, now.

HARRY. Okay, mate, calm –

GRACE. Howling, Harry, howling –

HARRY. Okay, you're upset and –

GRACE. I WILL NOT BE TOLD BY YOU. You're weak. You
are too weak. You've failed. You knew about the threats,
wolves, 'kids' whatever it is, you knew about it long ago and
did nothing. Give me the keys. NOW!

HARRY *hands the keys over to* GRACE.

DEE. Probably dogs, love. All domesticated dogs are descended
from wolves. Might be one wolf escaped from a zoo maybe
and several dogs have joined.

CHRIS. Hm.

DEE. Or it could be them. Ex-students. Grown-up kids. Bad
people. Ida, maybe.

CHRIS. Hm.

DEE. Yes, bad.

CHRIS. Hm.

DEE. Yeah, I know she's eleven but with her family? What
chance does she have? You know why they were moved here,
you know about her father – Is it worth all the effort of
defending people who could do something like this? Worth all
the effort of trying to work out why they've become like this?

CHRIS. Yes. Always.

DEE. Why? We're overpopulated as it is, why not give
evolution a helping hand and weed some of the bad seeds
out? Doesn't that make sense? What if the entire system, the
whole thing, love, what if it's all built on the lie that inside,
we're all essentially good and what if that's a naive idea on
a planet with limited resources –

CHRIS. Of course we should try to help people –

DEE. All people, Chris? People who'd do this kind of a thing?
People who want us dead – Cos there are people in the
world, Chris, who would smash these windows, take a
penknife and hack through our necks until our screams
became gurgles and –

CHRIS. Dee!?

DEE. I've seen these videos, these children have seen these videos, this is the world they live in, it's a world where niceness is weak and cruelty is power – This is what they feel – Out there in the dark – I see it in their eyes – It's a hard truth, Chris. A hard truth – Why won't you talk about what I said?

CHRIS....

DEE. Did you even hear it, did any of it go in or are you that set on avoiding it –

CHRIS. I heard it.

DEE. Well, you haven't replied, have you, love?

CHRIS....

DEE. Haven't responded apart from bundling me into a car, love, as if that'd be any safer –

CHRIS. Don't.

DEE....hey?

CHRIS. Call me that. Not at the moment. Not if we're going to... talk about this.

Another little pause.

DEE. But you agree, don't you? We should talk.

CHRIS. Mm.

DEE. Can you not make that sound, please. Can you use words instead.

CHRIS. Hm... I... think... the garden looks better with weeds. If we're talking about the big things then I like the weeds. I think it's prettier when it's... as God intended, so to speak.

DEE. That's not exactly / what I was –

CHRIS. I think it is. It's exactly what we should talk about. Because I've seen you at the rock out the back of the house with a scrubbing brush trying to keep the moss off it. I've seen you shaving your armpits and dying your hair. I've seen you attempting to manage unmanageable things and it's time to just let it all... develop. And that goes for people too, trust that we can all live through these things, cope with changes –

It's the constant attempt to control that's boring – The repetitive attempts, just let it all sprout and grow and change and rise and overcome and overpower and invade and permeate and everything. Let it be as it wants to be. Too many things try to restrict it all and if our cells, our own brain cells can turn against us then let's celebrate this out-of-control – You're right, we've stagnated because we're caught in this endless battle of trying to resist... growth.

DEE. Christopher.

CHRIS. You help me. You have always helped me. And I love you for that, it might be that you don't love me any more but everything in me *tends* towards you like weeds tend towards the sun. Every beating part of me is *for* you because I admire you –

DEE. Not now.

CHRIS. Yes, now.

DEE. I said bad things today –

CHRIS. No, you're trying to change things, really.

DEE. I ruined a little girl's dreams today.

CHRIS. No, you can't ruin someone else's dreams, that's not how it works.

DEE. The mould, in the corner of the bathroom, that's you ruining my dream / of it being clean.

CHRIS. Let it grow. Let it all grow. Let the roots push up the floorboards and the ivy crowd out those angle-poise lamps, I want your iPad crowded out with daisies and covered in moss, I want the marking to pile so high that mushrooms spore on the mounds of paper and make a rainforest of the living room –

DEE *kisses* CHRIS.

I thought you said –

DEE. I did. And I meant it. As much as I mean this, now.

DEE *kisses* CHRIS *again*.

CHRIS. But, what about the talk we need to have –

DEE. This is it. We're muddling through it.

CHRIS. It's probably because I've been so self-absorbed, I've basically been wearing my colon as a hat recently and I'm sorry –

DEE. Ugh, Chris.

CHRIS. You know what I mean, just fewer swear words –

DEE. Well, faith wouldn't be faith if it weren't constantly in crisis, would it?

CHRIS. Shouldn't that go for faith in people too?

DEE *kisses* CHRIS *again.*

DEE. How do you turn off the interior light?

CHRIS. Wait, I have to take my dog collar off –

DEE *barks like a dog.*

CHRIS *laughs and growls.*

This builds to a warped sound of chatter and hubbub and fear that could almost be the sound of a pack of wolves hunting.

GRACE. We need action, clear, decisive action, we need to barricade the windows, we need weapons, anything we can find and we need to organise, we need to send out a group to find a telephone and call for help and to search for Ellen and the Lewises and the vicar and his wife and PC Jones should go, not lead, but go and – And Mr King should lead them, he's a farmer, he'll know better than the rest of us – And for the benefit of those staying here, the rest of us, we need to reduce the – To speak freely, freedom of speech, we need to – to make sure that threats from inside are – are managed, I'm sure we all feel this, but people like – like Ferdy, Michael Button, Kelly Mann, the O'Connells perhaps, yes, we need to ask that they stay in a – a designated area, maybe a lockable designated – Cos we don't know, do we? We just don't know who or what or – And I think we should lock it, certainly watch it – Because the rest of us are good, hardworking and – and – we don't do bad things, do we?

A gunshot.

GRACE *is paralysed with horror.*

Ellen. Ellen, Ellen, lights, lights, lights, now, lights!!

A blackout.

What happened? What happened – / Oh, God, Lord, God protect us...

Another voice in the dark as HARRY *says:*

HARRY. It's just the fuse, mate, it's okay, it's –

HARRY*'s torch illuminates* TWO *covered in blood.*

Screams fill the hall and the torch falls to the ground.

FERDY. EVERYONE STOP! It's alright. It's okay. It's just Ida O'Connell.

FERDY *picks up the torch and illuminates himself.*

FERDY *shines the torch at* IDA.

IDA. Sss – Sss – ssss –

FERDY. Ida, it's Ferdy.

IDA. I'm sss-sss-sssorry, I'm sss-o sss –

FERDY. It's alright, no one's angry with you, Ida. Remember me? The big, crusty one from the caravan in the woods?

IDA. You eat sss-sssquirrels –

FERDY. I'm gonna stop the bleeding. Can you be brave?

IDA *nods.*

FERDY *carefully takes* IDA*'s hand and applies pressure.*

IDA *stifles a whimper.*

Okay?

IDA....okay.

FERDY. Looks like glass stuck in here.

IDA. Yeah.

FERDY. Not a wolf breaking in then.

IDA. I ss-ssmass – Broke the glass.

FERDY. Alright.

IDA. Sss-ssorry.

FERDY. It's okay.

IDA. I juss-ss – I needed help.

FERDY. And you asked for it. Which is good. You did a good thing. Now, keep hold of your hand for me. Keep applying pressure, that's right, that's good. I'm gonna need to speak to some people, make sure no more accidents happen and then I'll be back. Okay?

IDA *nods*.

Someone unplug those lights, flick the fuse for me, and get the power back on.

The stage manager signals that the job is accepted.

Now, Grace.

TWO *has gone from portraying* IDA *applying pressure to her hand to* GRACE, *wringing her hands in blind fear.*

GRACE....

FERDY. Grace, deep breath. Okay?

GRACE. Um, um –

FERDY. That wasn't Ellen. It was Ida. Wasn't it?

GRACE. I, don't – I –

FERDY. Believe me, I've seen gunshot wounds before. I'll treat her hand in a minute. Then you and me –

GRACE. But Ellen – My Ellen –

FERDY. We're gonna make a plan and find Ellen. But only when you've calmed down, okay?

GRACE *nods*.

We'll get help. We'll find her together. We'll make sure she's okay. Understood?

GRACE *looks at* FERDY. FERDY *meets her eyes*.

Now, that was a gunshot. But it came from uphill, Lewis Farm way, and if there are any wolves about, what do you think she'd do?

GRACE (*quiet*). Shoot them.

FERDY. That's right, she'd shoot them and she's a good shot, let me tell you. Do you think your Ellen would be anywhere around Lewis Farm?

GRACE *shakes her head*.

No, she's not one for barbed wire and muck, is she?

GRACE....

FERDY. We'll find her.

GRACE *looks at* FERDY.

GRACE. Why are you being nice to me?

FERDY. Because you're frightened. And when you're frightened, it's easy to make things worse and worse till you've made your own prison. I've been frightened. I've made my own prisons before. But it's okay now. Because we're all going to work together. Yes?

GRACE. Yes.

FERDY. Those cakes you made, they'd go nicely with a brew around now, wouldn't they? Help us think nice and clearly. You know where the kitchen is, don't you?

GRACE. Yes.

FERDY. Thanks, Grace.

GRACE *is evidently speaking to herself in the darkness*.

GRACE. I'll just – I'll just – Just tea and – and cakes and we can all um – Kitchen so – so –

Suddenly, the lights come back on and GRACE *sees something*.

ONE. There, in the kitchen, Grace finds herself face to face with the one thing she's always feared.

TWO *begins to move and preen and then to dance.*

It's her daughter, Ellen.

TWO*'s dance gradually expresses more and more
frustration.*

ELLEN*'s music blasts and we realise that* ELLEN *is the one
dancing. It is the dance of someone trying to rearrange the
bones of their body, trying to change the world, the dance
that people have always danced here and the brand new
dance of a unique person all at the same time.* GRACE
watches, terrified, delighted, amazed, furuious…

GRACE. What the HELL are you doing? Where have you been?

ELLEN *stands, shocked.*

What will people say? Do you have any idea how
embarrassing this is for me? For us?

ELLEN *is upset, she makes towards* GRACE.

No, don't come any closer, Ellen, just… The dog's dead. You
left the back door open when you ran off. Terrified everyone
in the village – Running away, Ellen? From me?

Is this something you do? This – This kind of music? I thought
you liked nice music, not…

ELLEN. No, no, yeah, no, my body's like, yeah, it's wrong
for – ?

GRACE. No. Your body's perfect. Your dancing is perfect.
You're perfect. I missed you.

FERDY. Right, Pope, King, O'Connells and Harry, you're with
me. Everyone else, keep checking your phones. Any signal,
call the emergency services first.

GRACE. Ferdy?

FERDY. Was there a landline in here? Have you seen a –

GRACE. Ferdy? I found Ellen. She's here.

FERDY *stops.*

FERDY. Good. That's… really good. But the vicar, the teacher –

GRACE. Actually, Ferdy. Ellen says it's sunrise and… well, maybe we all just need a bit of fresh air.

FERDY. Fresh air – ?

GRACE. Ellen and I think we should open the doors. What do you think?

FERDY flinches – becoming aware of the eyes on him.

ELLEN. Yeah, yeah, no, Ferdy, we should all just see. I mean, I've not done any research or anything but I don't think wolves… or whoever, I don't think they'd come for all of us. Together.

FERDY. All of us.

ELLEN. Yeah, we should just, like, meet them, you know. Head on. Stop hiding.

FERDY sniffs. He sniffs the air nearer the audience. It's not intimidating, it's not aggressive, just odd.

Cos, I mean, what's the alternative? Sit in here and argue and – and –

FERDY (*by way of agreement*). All of you should open the doors.

ELLEN. Yeah, no, we should, yeah. Mum?

FERDY (*retreating*). You can all… Yeah.

GRACE. Harry. Here are the keys. Sorry for what I… I don't want to be that person, I was… I think it's fair to say that I was… But Ellen's here now and is anyone else feeling claustrophobic? I mean, I'm feeling claustrophobic. Anyway, here they are. Thanks, Harry.

GRACE gives the keys to ONE, who becomes HARRY as she takes them. TWO goes from GRACE's hand-wringing to IDA maintaining pressure.

HARRY (*steeling himself*). Alright, mate… Alright.

IDA. Sss-ssorry, but I want to help. I want to help open the doors with you.

HARRY. Ida, mate, it's dangerous –

IDA. When people tell the ss-ss– (*Deep breath.*) story. I want it to be good.

HARRY. Okay, mate. Ready?

IDA. Let's sss – (*Deep breath.*) Let's – (*Deep breath.*) see what happens next.

Epilogue

ONE *holds out a slightly trembling hand.*

TWO *takes it.*

ONE. [*Name of FOH or village-hall manager*]? Could you open the doors for us?

The keys are passed back to the FOH or village-hall manager.

TWO. Thanks.

Hopefully the doors are opened during the following text. Hopefully the air rushes in.

ONE. Stars fading as the sky brightens, bit less mist in the valley this morning. The sun hasn't broken the brow of the hill yet, but it's coming. And as the doors of our village hall are opened, it all looks how it must have looked when it was truly, properly, wild. Doesn't it?

TWO. That's the end of our play. Thanks, everyone.

Perhaps we play a song that we all love as everyone leaves.

Perhaps, outside, everyone shares tea and cake.

Finally, whether witnessed by the audience or not, ONE *and* TWO *destroy the circle of soil and the ritual of this play is completed through its destruction.*

The End.